Herald to Chaos

EARL H. ROVIT

Herald

THE NOVELS OF

to Chaos

Elizabeth Madox Roberts

UNIVERSITY *of* KENTUCKY PRESS

*The publication of this book has been made possible partly
through a grant from the Margaret Voorhies Haggin Trust,
established in memory of her husband, James Ben Ali Haggin.*

FOR
MY MOTHER AND FATHER

Acknowledgments

ANY THOUGHTFUL ACT—and this ought to include an act of criticism like my following study of Elizabeth Madox Roberts —is the result of a congeries of influences and determinations upon the actor. As the actor in this present situation I am deeply conscious of the enormous emotional and intellectual debts I have incurred in the making of this book. Were life so constituted that such debts need be repaid in similar coin, I would be spiritually bankrupt many times over. As it is, this preface affords me the opportunity of making a partial acknowledgment of my debts and of offering this book as partial payment.

My most comprehensive debt is to my wife, Honey Weisenfeld Rovit, who has suffered the total weight of this book—and so much else besides. The rigor of her critical intelligence has never faltered, but neither has her innocent belief in my capacity to do better work than I thought possible. Without her insistent criticism and her equally insistent faith, this book would have been far different.

My most obvious debts are to Professors Edward A. Post and Edward C. Wagenknecht of Boston University, who first

Acknowledgments

stimulated my interest in Miss Roberts' work, and who followed up their stimulation with wise and critical guidance.

To Barbara Tunnel and Dwight Anderson of Louisville, who shared with me the recollections of their intimate friendship with and love for Miss Roberts, yielding me an image of the living personality behind her written words.

To the following teachers, colleagues, and friends, whose brains I erratically picked and who need be in no way responsible, unless they so choose, for what I have done with their well-ordered values and judgments: Morris Bein, Angelo Bertocci, Charles Breslin, Lee Allan Burress, Frances Brownell Burstein, William Ekstrom, Leo Hertzel, Edmond Schlesinger, Martin Stevens, John Tagliabue, Harvey Curtis Webster.

To my students at Bates College and the University of Louisville, who have suffered my confusions with patience and who have helped me far more than they have ever understood.

To the Administration and Research Fund Committee of the University of Louisville for encouragement, moral and financial, in the preparation of this book.

To the directors and staffs of the libraries of the University of Louisville, the University of Kentucky, Harvard University, the Filson Club, the Bureau of Manuscripts Division of the Library of Congress, and the Henry M. Hacker Educational Center for their courteous and efficient offices.

To Frida Schlesinger, who corrected proof with laborious patience and loving discrimination.

To the editors of *The Mississippi Quarterly*, who published materials which I have since reworked for this book.

To the editors of The Viking Press for permission to quote from Miss Roberts' publications which they hold in

Acknowledgments

copyright. To Ivor Roberts, executor of the Elizabeth Madox Roberts estate, for permission to quote from her unpublished papers.

None of the above ought to be held responsible for any of the gross errors or stupidities herein committed. These last are all my own. It is my hope, however, that something of the shape and rhythm of this essay in criticism may reflect worthily on the memory of my late and very dear friend, Richard G. MacLaughlin, who died too soon to fulfill what would have been a rich and productive life. In his memory I humbly offer my book.

Louisville
June, 1960

Contents

CHAPTER ONE

Introduction

THERE ARE AT LEAST TWO justifications, I believe, for a detailed study of the novels of Elizabeth Madox Roberts. For reasons which are generally unrelated to her intrinsic literary merit, she has failed to receive the critical attention which the scope and texture of her fictions deserve.[1] Her reputation as a novelist—an imposing one in the late 1920's and early 1930's —has steadily declined until today her name is relatively unknown, save as a Kentucky "regionalist" with peculiar stylistic eccentricities. This study is, in the first place, an attempt to make some partial restitution for what seems to me unwarranted critical neglect.

Secondly, I think that a close study of her novels possesses an additional, although less obvious, interest as a means of increasing our understanding of contemporary cultural history. It seems to me that Elizabeth Madox Roberts was keenly sensitive to the major stresses and ambiguities of twentieth-century American life and thought. She was profoundly aware of the difficulties of maintaining stable values in a time when things are in the saddle and space-time is in explosion; she recognized early the irreconcilable conflict between the democratic ideal of individualism and the encroaching forces of collectivism. As a novelist, Miss Roberts dealt imaginatively and successfully with the manifold problems of creating fiction in a world where all our facts have turned into fictions. She accepted the full challenge of modern uncertainty, and, within the flux of our contemporary shadowland of values, established a strong and positive structure of artistic and human faith. I shall further suggest that among her novels which incarnate this faith we may find some of the major fictional achievements of our century.

ELIZABETH MADOX ROBERTS was born on October 30, 1881, in Perryville, Kentucky; she was the second of eight children born to Mary Elizabeth Brent and Simpson Roberts, surveyor, farmer, schoolmaster.[2] Most of her childhood was spent in Springfield, Kentucky, a small town on the banks of the Salt River to which her family moved in 1887. Except for four years in Covington, Kentucky (1896-1900) while she attended high school, and her years at the University of Chicago (1917-1921), Springfield was her nominal headquarters and home throughout her life. She seems to have begun attendance at the State College of Kentucky (later, the University of Kentucky) in September, 1900, but she was forced, probably by poor health, to return to Springfield before the end of the first semester. Ill health was to plague her inces-

Introduction

santly for the next sixteen years and for the last ten years of her life, effectively thwarting her personal plans and ambitions, causing her a good deal of pain and discomfort, and so emphasizing her native sensitivity that the channel of artistic expression ultimately became her predominant mode of communication with the outside world.[3] The immediate consequence of this early "frailty" was her surrender of a college education. After this, she remained in or near Springfield until 1910, employed sporadically as a schoolteacher.

Between 1910 and 1916 she lived intermittently with her sister Luellen in Colorado, and as her health gradually improved, began to work seriously with poetry; she published some short pieces in magazines and had her first volume, *In the Great Steep's Garden*, privately printed in 1915.[4] By January, 1917, she was able to enter the freshman class at the University of Chicago. Whether this was the resolution of a long-brooded-upon desire or a sudden impulse is not certain; at any rate, at the age of thirty-six she was suddenly exposed to what may have been the most stimulating literary atmosphere in America at that time. She took courses under Robert Morss Lovett and the famous medievalist Edith Rickerts; she joined the University Poetry Club, becoming its president in her senior year and entering wholeheartedly into its inner circle of student-writers—a group which included Glenway Wescott, Monroe Wheeler, Janet Lewis, and Yvor Winters. As a college student she published seventeen poems, one in *Poetry*, two in *Atlantic Monthly*, the others scattered in various little magazines. She had a limited access to Harriet Monroe's salon, where the great and popular in the literary world touched as they passed through Chicago. Although it is impossible to assess the influence of these Chicago years on her basic thinking, there seems little doubt that they were of

3

tremendous importance in giving her a sense of intellectual self-confidence and in introducing her into a community of thought where questions of artistic technique and ideals were treated as central rather than peripheral interests.

After receiving her degree, she returned to Springfield to settle into a routine of writing which was uninterrupted save by physical disability until her death. Her first major collection of poetry, *Under the Tree,* was published in 1922.[5] In the same year she began work on *The Time of Man,* which was completed and published in 1926. This novel met with immediate publishing success, rapidly running through several printings, and being chosen as a Book-of-the-Month Club selection. The book reviewers voiced an enthusiastic welcome to the new novelist and Miss Roberts was thrust into firstline critical recognition. Almost as soon as the writing of this novel was finished, she was at work on *My Heart and My Flesh,* which was published a year later. The next five years saw five more volumes: *Jingling in the Wind* (1928); *The Great Meadow* (1930); *Under the Tree* (rev. ed., 1930); *A Buried Treasure* (1931); and *The Haunted Mirror* (short stories, 1932). She was awarded the John Reed Memorial Prize by *Poetry* in 1928 and the Caroline Sinkler Memorial Prize by the Poetry Society of South Carolina in 1931. In 1932 her story, "The Sacrifice of the Maidens," was given the O. Henry Second Prize Award, and in 1933 she was offered an honorary degree (Litt.D.) by Russell Sage College for her achievements in American letters. With the publication of *He Sent Forth a Raven* in 1935, however, her popularity—both critical and commercial—began to plummet.

The royalties which she had earned with her earlier volumes—two Literary Guild selections and the movie rights to *The Great Meadow*—swiftly diminished. Her health also

Introduction

deteriorated, forcing her to leave Springfield during the raw Kentucky winters, which put an additional drain on her financial resources. It was probably at this time that she began to suffer severely from what was later diagnosed as Hodgkin's disease. She continued to write, however, expanding a sketch written in 1933 to *Black Is My Truelove's Hair* (1938). Her third volume of poetry, *Song in the Meadow*, was published in 1940, and she lived long enough to correct the proofs for *Not By Strange Gods* (1941), her second collection of short stories.[6] She died in Orlando, Florida, on March 13, 1941.

ALTHOUGH HER FIRST NOVEL was not published until she was forty-five years old, Elizabeth Madox Roberts was by no means a "primitive" artist. Indeed, she was almost completely the reverse—a highly self-conscious aesthetician and craftsman. Scattered throughout her journals and letters are persistent efforts to discover what her own personal limitations as an artist were, and how best to bend these limitations to the production of fine art. In her journal she notes: "Two ways seemed always open to me as one having such environmental influences as mine, and such physical and mental equipment. One the way of satire, the other the way of symbolism working through poetic realism."[7] The way of satire is illustrated only in her fantasy, *Jingling in the Wind*; in all her other novels, as well as in the most successful sections of *Jingling in the Wind*, the sustained note of composition is "symbolism working through poetic realism." What she meant by this is clarified in the following:

I will tell you why we continually go back to realism in art. Somewhere there is a connection between the world of the mind and the outer order—It is the secret of the contact that we are after, the point, the moment of union. We faintly sense the one and we know as faintly the other, but there is a point at which they come together, and we can never know the whole of reality until we know these two completely. And so we pursue first the one and then the other. We probe deeper and deeper into the world of sense and experience and we say "Now I have it, it is thus" . . . and presently it is seen that we haven't it yet and we make another try with a newer realism or some of us try for it the other way around.

Elsewhere she succinctly summarizes her characteristic mode of approach, saying: "I have tried for great precision in rendering sensuous contacts—the points where poetry touches life."

Miss Roberts was early nurtured on the idealistic philosophy of Bishop Berkeley, her father's favorite philosopher, and this influence is a pervasive tincture in her thinking. The sovereignty of mind, or spirit, over unformed matter is basic to her understanding of life and distinctively colors her concept of the artistic process. "Life is from within, and thus the noise outside is a wind blowing in a mirror."[8] Until the life "outside" becomes comprehended within—until sensation is transformed into idea, or poetry—the outside life is as meaningless as "a wind blowing in a mirror." Such a philosophic idealism could easily lead to abortive ends. It could constrict itself into an imprisoning solipsism which denies validity to anything outside one's own fantasy projections. It can distort the meaning of life into anything the egotistical assigner of meanings wants it to mean, and by denying a reality principle, end in insanity or fatal frustration. By cutting the deep roots between experience and values, it can cause moral paralysis,

6

Introduction

perversion, and intellectual suicide. If there is no connection between the world of the mind and the outer order, the mind has only itself to feed upon and growth is impossible. But Miss Roberts was aware of the dangers of unqualified idealism to the artist and to the human being, and she sought assiduously to avoid those dangers.

Her aim, both personal and artistic, was to focus on those points "where poetry touches life"—where mind and matter, idea and sensation, vision and fact, intermingle, shape and are shaped, and produce conjointly a flood of identity within the perceiving spirit, wherein the outer order is creatively absorbed and the world of the mind comprises a new universe. This, she believed, was the area where her art could operate most effectively—where the artistic symbol, itself a fusion of idea and thing, could communicate that which could not be communicated by any other means.

She was dedicated to her art because she saw it as a handmaiden to a greater energy—for her, the elemental energy in life—love. For though she writes that "life is from within" and the noise outside negligible, she qualifies this world-denying isolation by adding: "But love is a royal visitor which that proud ghost, the human spirit, settles in elegant chambers and serves with the best." And, as will become clear in the examination of her specific novels, "love" for Miss Roberts is not only the outgoing desire which moves man to accept from, and share with, other men the unique selfness which one has; but, even more basically, the force itself which brings man to the points where poetry touches life, where one's very selfness is created. The moments of union—the vital experiences of truth, of virtue, of beauty—which mark the successive spirals of growth for the individual spirit, are themselves love-created. The absence of love is

7

for Miss Roberts, in a many-layered sense, always synonymous with death.

Her novels, then, served a twofold purpose. For her, personally, they were metaphors of experience—love creations through which her own inner spirit could expand, absorb the materials of itself, and integrate itself into a new and more vital level of growth. But because she also possessed a deep sense of responsibility to the body of mankind of which she was a part, they are also love offerings to mankind—symbols of her experience which she contributed in the hope that other men might use them for their own growth. Both purposes are eloquently pointed to in her statement: ("It is the function of art to enlarge one's experience, to add to man more tolerance, more forgiveness, to increase one's hold on all the out-lying spaces which are little realized in the come and go of every day.")

CHAPTER TWO

Moments of Union

THE TIME OF MAN (1926): A Modern Odyssey

ELIZABETH MADOX ROBERTS' first novel was begun in the summer of 1922 and published in August, 1926. However, like most of her work, the actual writing commenced only after a number of years spent in brooding over the material and striving to focus on a major comprehensive symbol. In her journal notes she writes: "It was, I think, in the summer of 1919 that I began to think of the wandering tenant farmer of our region as offering a symbol for an Odyssy [*sic*] of Man as a wanderer buffeted about by the fates and weathers." Her use of the Homeric reference is not by any means haphazard. Several statements in her private papers reveal her conviction that a modern realistic novel can be infused with the qualities of classical epic. "The only subjects worthy of permanent consideration," she wrote, "are the fundamental passions, or instincts. Homeric themes of blood and waste and death. . . . Of life." In another journal entry, she reports being "struck" on reading Samuel, Books I and II, with the possibilities of what she termed "the cluster of epic story." In a note on Caldwell's *God's Little Acre* she remarks:

Interesting material not well handled. The colloquial tone of the main body of the prose lowers the level of it. . . .

The material is superior to the handling, which, being "realism" was beneath the level of the colossal,—Warlike, Homeric, blood-and-anger thrust of the whole cause. . . . The loss of dignity in the method, the reader's danger of being lost or confused by the detail, will exclude many from following the work to the end. A more dignified or symbolic handling would save it.

It should be recognized at the outset, of course, that Miss Roberts had no intention of parodying the more superficial characteristics of the epic form. She has no invocations to the Muses; she does not begin her action *in medias res*; she has neither superhuman hero, nor animated personifications of godly forces. Her main effort is devoted to the presentation of a "heroic" character, engaged in the epic struggle for life against the fatal forces of nature. The poetic perception of truth offered by ancient Greek cosmology had to be revitalized to satisfy the exigencies of twentieth-century thought and literature. The rigid classical line between man and nature—between Odysseus and the catastrophes which beset him—had to be blurred to do justice to our contemporary understanding of the enigmatic interaction of consciousness and chaos.

Her choice of hero is dramatically un-Homeric—a fourteen-year-old girl, a child of the earth, uncultured and of no prominence. The Greek prince of many guiles, Odysseus, wanders for ten years, encountering and subduing colossal obstacles; Ellen Chesser wanders for roughly twenty years, grubbing at the very roots of life to sustain her existence. Odysseus returns finally to his own royal hall to live in peace and grandeur, but Ellen Chesser lives at the end as at the beginning, wandering the roads, struggling anew and anew to keep life within her. Obviously the concept of "hero" has undergone a radical change between Homer's *Odyssey* and Miss Roberts' *The Time of Man*.

The classical hero enters the action of his story full-blown; he is himself—Odysseus, Hector, Achilles, Oedipus. There is no obligation on the author to build up his character by portraying how he came to be what he is, and his noble nature will be inherent in the nobility of his lineage. And the stage on which this hero performs is an exalted one: his battles are for kingdoms, his love affairs are with princesses, and his defeats are signals for universal mourning and desolation. But if the modern author wants to portray a noble character of heroic qualities, he must make this character noble and heroic in a probable life situation, and he must precisely assess the forces which limit the range of his character's self-determined actions. Miss Roberts was committed to realism as the only mode in which she could communicate successfully. Thus, her major problem in attempting to achieve epic strength in *The Time of Man* centers on her main character. Ellen Chesser must somehow incarnate the highest virtues of humanity while being, at the same time, a convincing representative of the "poor white" southern tenant-farmer class.

First, Miss Roberts establishes and keeps constantly before the reader the spectacular panorama of nature as a continuous

11

cyclical process. Ellen Chesser's daily life is swallowed up in agricultural occupations: setting out tobacco, feeding turkeys, milking her heifer, gathering eggs, helping with the plowing. The succession of seasons, inexorable and merciless, acts out in this setting the role played in ancient epic story by blind and pitiless fate. Harvesttime follows seedtime, and seedtime follows harvesttime; the baby cries for attention, and the heifer noses the front gate to be milked; the demand of the land and the animals must be satisfied. The eternal onward going of time thrusts the child into adolescence, into maturity, into age, calling forth new life out of birth throes, and settling old life back into the earth to become one with it. The "time of man" is felt in motion, without beginning or end:

"No plow iron ever cut this-here hill afore, not in the whole time of man." Henry said.

"The time of man," as a saying fell over and over in Ellen's mind. The strange men that lived here before our men, a strange race doing things in strange ways, and other men before them, and before again. Strange feet walking on a hillside for some purpose she could never think. Wondering and wondering she laid stones on her altar.

Ellen Chesser is just one of the "children of the earth," infinite in number, alike in general pattern: working, loving, wanting, and always, in the end, dying. The desertion of her lover plunges her to the brink of suicide, but nature asserts itself in her and lays new growth over the deep wounded places:

The field had been neglected for the summer rains had lasted overlong. She ceased to think of any day before this day or of any task before this. Each plant freed of weeds was something liberated, but another stood trammelled, the same endlessly snared, the same, until she tramped a treadmill and her thought was

clodded with earth. The sun was warm on her aching shoulders
and her strong knees quivered with the strain. As she plied the
hoe a quick image of the year, a season, from planting to cutting
and stripping, stood forth as if it were in the soil, a design, all
finished and set apart. The design of the grass roots matted with
the soil lay under her eyes, complete forever, varying in every
detail but forever the same. The hoe came down over and over,
no two blows exactly alike but no varying in the form. The year
stood plainly designed, one with the grass and the dust, a certain
year, formed with beginning and end, planting and cutting, gay
laughing and places to go. She had said happy things and they
had seemed to have meanings, and people had said things back to
her, things she had kept in mind to smile at afterward. All now
lay in the form of the year. A little nick in the bright edge of the
hoe twinkled in and out of the brown of the earth. The hoe cut
in half its depth or cut in more, and the grains of earth fell airily
against the dull upper part. The year began to turn, a form moving lightly upon itself, but she minded nothing of the year, for her
body had changed, and the hoe and the soil now cut each other
sharply, visible and near. "Jonas," she said over and over. It was
a name, that was all, a name for something that was gone.

I quote this passage in its entirety because it illustrates
Miss Roberts' use of rhythmic devices to intensify the emotional effect of her prose. The repetition of constructions,
the series of balanced cadences in this passage create a pattern
of sound which reflects the endless recurrences of nature
—"varying in detail but forever the same." Miss Roberts
keeps the seasonal changes of the landscape constantly before
the reader's eyes, employing the images of nature not as a
mere background, but as an integral part of the action. The
passage of time is always denoted in terms of weather, crops,
or landscape:

Henry Chesser drove the mower up and down the clover field,
cutting the hay for Mr. Bodine.

Herald to Chaos

She liked to sit in the corn after it grew waist-high or more.

The creek was almost dry in the August drouth. A green scum stood on the stagnant pools of water in the small basins. . . .

The twilights were falling earlier day by day, and strange shadows, different from the summer-cast shadows, slanted under the locust trees.

It was another year. Late May sounds and smells spread over the plowed field, the tobacco field . . . ready again for plants.

The grass was high and full with seeds and the white clover was in bloom—late June.

The first of January came with mild thawing weather after a season of freezing and snow.

It was a mild March day, cool and clear, with winds worrying the hillside brush and leaping off across the farms in a great rush. . . .

The literary effect of this constant awareness of the patterned flux of nature is not unlike that of the fixed cosmos of the Greek world, or the divinely ordained order of the Elizabethan world. And the human drama enacted in an involvement with this principle must, by necessity, attain epic significance. It is this that F. L. Janney is pointing to in his comment on *The Time of Man*: "Seen as they are against the seemingly eternal background of seed times and harvest, the story of their lives derives a pathos and poignancy, an epic quality, which attaches to those who silently pursue their lonely ways down a road ending at last in the defeat of their hopes and in oblivion."[1] I will have cause to disagree with Janney over his words "pathos" and "defeat," but I think that his perception is otherwise sound. F. W. Knickerbocker comes, I believe, to a more solid conclusion in the following comment: "Such a rendering of human life as part of the great

14

process of nature recalls Wordsworth's *Michael*, Hardy's *Tess*, or Reymont's *Peasants*. These figures are all emblems of the common lot. And so Ellen's wandering becomes a symbol of 'that whole time of man' on which she sometimes broods."[2]

The point that should be stressed here is that Ellen Chesser is a real "emblem of the common lot," a symbol of man caught up in the even flow of nature, and that Miss Roberts achieves this symbolism by stripping Ellen Chesser of every refinement of culture not absolutely essential to that which makes her a human being. She is, in a sense, the lowest common denominator of mankind; she is poor, uneducated, one of those who are "sown thus as wildings." Miss Roberts chooses her hero to represent that which is most fundamental to the definition of a human being, rather than that which is finest among human beings; to her, as to Emerson, "representative man" is not the champion of classical times, but the average man. Miss Roberts' epic struggle is between an everyman, shorn of all save humanity, and the eternal powers of nature.

A plot summary of the novel will focus on the harsh circumstances and the heartbreaking incidents which envelop Ellen Chesser from beginning to end. Traveling in wagons from farm to farm, staying to work for a little while, and then moving on, the Chesser family settles in a tenant house at Hep Bodine's when Ellen is fourteen. There life for Ellen is composed of housework, gathering firewood, setting out tobacco, and, when all the chores are done, running free. Two years later, the Chessers move on to the Wakefield farm, where Ellen makes friends of her own age, acquires some responsibility, falls in love, and is spurned by her lover. At the next place, the Orkey farm, Ellen marries Jasper Kent, a tenant farmer who has become unjustly implicated in a barn burning. In the succeeding fifteen years, Ellen has six children, one of whom dies, and she changes her home three times. Then Jasper Kent's old incendiary history rises up against him, forcing him to leave again for a new place. The novel ends with the whole family packed into a wagon along with the meager household goods: "They went a long way while the moon was still high above the trees, stopping only at some creek to water the beasts. They asked no questions of the way but took their own turnings."

Such a summary of the external action of *The Time of Man* may seem to justify Janney's "pathos" and "defeat," but these events are not the subject of the novel, which is a spiritual Odyssey. Its theme is the development of character, and it ends not in defeat but in triumph.

We meet Ellen in the very first sentence of the novel, writing her name in the air with her finger, secretive and reserved in her childishness, but alert to everything around her. In a journal note, Miss Roberts writes: "The plan of the book is founded upon additions. The intention was to begin with the least that one could handle, scarcely more than the breath of life in the throat, and slowly to add minute particle after minute particle until a being with life experience should be built together." And, according to this principle, Ellen is developed—painfully, gradually, cumulatively. In her past she holds idyllic memories of Tessie West of the wonderful stories and the geography book; before her lies her whole life and a goal, deeply lying and vague, of a pretty house and security. She makes an abortive attempt to rejoin Tessie and her past, and then settles into an apathy of submission to life, the last deep sleep of childhood prior to the awakening into adolescence. In the Joe Trent episode the quickening of sex within her makes her aware of herself in a much more complicated

16

Moments of Union

way than can be expressed by tracing her name in the air:
"I'm lovely now. . . . It's unknowen how lovely I am. It runs
up through my sides and into my shoulders, warm, and ne'er
thing else is any matter. . . . It's unknowen how lovely I am,
unknowen." Thus, when the torments of adolescence, "the
perpetual sadness of youth," begin to beset her with anxious
questionings of the value of life, her personality has by this
time coalesced sufficiently so that out of the depths of her
felt identity comes an irrefutable answer to the tormenting
questions. The *how* and *what for* are shadowed into silence
by the triumphal realization of *AM*. And this answer is more
firmly established with the episode of Judge Gowan's tombstone and her realization that life is unchallengeably more
wonderful than death.

As Ellen's confidence in herself increases, she becomes
able to submerge her identity in an anonymous group, surrendering her individuality to the group in return for the
strength and security which her membership affords her:
"Five shapes were thumping the dry road with their feet,
stumbling a little, five abreast now and now drifting into
forms like those the stars made in the sky. It was here that
she felt them become six, herself making part of the forms,
herself merged richly with the design." As Miss Roberts
notes in her journals: "This is the high pitch of youth. Here
is the social being which scarcely divides itself from the
group, which loves broadly through the entire troop of girls
and boys." The peak of this period is reached in the harvest-
dance scene:

She would not care if the dance had her or if it carried her
away into the dark of the woods or over the river. She gave herself
up to the dance not caring if the end of it never came. It swirled
around her confusion and plucked it into greater chaos. She let

17

the dance do what it would, and if it asked for her mouth she gave that, now careless and willing, or if it wanted her laugh or her smile or her arms. The wind blew and she felt as if she turned about in the center of a great wind, the other persons of the dance being but arms of the wind or limbs or the wind's ribbons or clothing. Her own mouth was in the wind, blown with its currents, ready for any gale, curving to any kiss that came to it. Then the wind was fraying the beech sand and blinding her eyes. . . . A great cloud rolled over the sky and the moon went out. Dust and dead leaves poured across the air. The dance had melted away into the certainty of the wind.

And just as the "certainty" of the wind destroys the wonderful "chaos" of the dance, so the certainty of life plucks the dancers, one by one, out of the pattern, individuating the members of the group. The first loss of this youthful security in anonymity for Ellen is felt when Jonas confesses his sin to her:

Jonas was troubled and his thought went far from her and had another center, gathering around his hurt. He wanted to be beside her but he wanted her there to share his pain, and she hated his pain for a moment. A part of him was gone and in the loss she was confused in a crossing of demands, denials, and finalities. Something was lost to her.

Jonas comes to her because she is Ellen Chesser, not because she is one of the dancers in the wind; and she feels both love and compassion for him, not as one of her friends, but as the unique being that her love has singled out. This is the point at which Ellen begins to achieve a true individuality.

The climax of this love affair is reached in a remarkable scene in which Miss Roberts uses a fire kindled with two kinds of wood to symbolize the slow beginnings and the passionate fusing of love:

18

Moments of Union

[She] laid two sticks on the fire, an ash piece and a piece of sycamore, and they lay darkly together for a few moments to enkindle. . . . The sticks lay together in the bed of the fire for a little and then sprang into first flames, bright, unheated, and new, uncertain, leaping higher and sinking away, but leaping brightly again. . . . The fire burned brightly now, the sycamore log and the ash, their flames blended into one flame and one light. . . .

By the renewed light of the fire he looked at her anew. She felt his gaze and his hands searching her for her beauty and she felt her beauty grow more full and rich when he called to it, and it became something which they held and owned together.

Shortly afterward, Cassie MacMurtrie discovers that her husband has been unfaithful to her for two years, and she hangs herself. Since Ellen is one of the first to enter the house, she has to answer under oath at the coroner's inquest whether she knows any reason why Cassie might have committed suicide. But Ellen can understand only life—filled as she is with her love and her sense of tingling self; she cannot understand death at all.

Ellen's spirit receives its first major blow when Jonas Prather deserts. She is in a state of dissociation from herself and life around her: "She came down from the pens knowing that all her beauties, assembled, standing around her, serene and proud, were standing about a great hollow inner space. In her body, in her breast, there was gathering a void, and it was spreading past her power to hold it." As the realization of her inner loss becomes more clear, she is shaken by a lust to kill—to revenge herself on her betrayer. The conjunction of themes is worth noting here as an illustration of Miss Roberts' characteristic techniques. Ellen had instinctively associated Scott MacMurtrie's affair with kinetic sensations of "lice"— sensations which she had earlier developed in her experience of shame before Mrs. Bodine and which she had trusted as

19

directional signals in her relations to Joe Trent and Sebe Townley. Thus she is somatically prepared for the violence of Cassie's suicide, but, innocent of any similar deprivation of love, she can hardly understand its motivation. After Jonas' desertion, the scene of the hanging is replayed in her consciousness, but this time with shocking immediacy and wholehearted empathy. She does discover an alternate solution to Cassie's self-destruction, but only after reliving to the depths Cassie's hell.

She withdraws into herself, seeking there for the inner stability of "Here I am." After the family leaves the Wakefield farm and moves to the Orkey place, her snug raintight room and her locked trunk symbolize her closing off of all outside contacts:

Ellen felt the snugness of the night, the dark outside, the falling wet, the dry security of the indoors, so that in her room, shut away from the elements, she felt the security to be within herself as if she were detached by the prison-like whiteness of the dry walls from her own memories, to begin her being anew; she had never before known this detachment from the immediacy of the weather. . . . Ellen found a delight in the snug dry room into which the rain could not come. . . . Her bed stood along one wall and a small wooden trunk which she had bought from the peddler stood along another. The key of the trunk lay on the shelf. . . . It was a pleasure to lock the chest and slip the key onto the high shelf where it lay out of sight.

Her father breaks his leg and she is forced to take his place in the fields. She merges her hurt spirit with the earth, for she "could not give delight . . . to a muslin or a frill now, her mind one with the wants of the fields, with the beasts and the plowed trenches." But time and life assert themselves, and Jonas is gradually absorbed into her memory as a fact no longer able to wound. She begins to place Jasper Kent's money in her trunk for safekeeping, and this fact signals the beginning of her return to life.[3] Finally, after the burning of the barn when Jasper is forced to flee with his savings, she is once more open to life, capable once more of being hurt to the very core of herself, but capable also of sharing her love: "The chest was no longer locked for it was empty of any treasure. Its key lay on the floor and its lid stood open, waiting, and as she passed into her room and closed the door behind her to sit for an hour or more, her waiting breath whispered, 'He will come.'"

Ellen is mature now in her knowledge of herself. Jasper returns to marry her, and in their new farm she bears two children and settles herself into the pattern made long before at the time of her hurt withdrawal from life: "The land was hard and rough and she must take what she could out of the bitter soil." She still thinks of "a place vaguely set among the trees, the consummation of some deeply-lying dream, a house looking toward some wide valley," but the arch of her spirit has learned a suppleness in dealing with life's offerings, no matter how far removed they may be from the level of her dreams or even expectations. Thus she is able not only to survive her continued poverty, the pitiful death of her last child, and Jasper's blatant infidelity, but she is able to transform such meager sustenance into strength and radiant love.

Long before the final departure of the family when Ellen has no need "to ask questions of the way," she has become solidified for the reader as something more than a pawn of the mercurial fates which buffet her about. She has been established as a growing active personality, accepting the brute circumstances of life, but forcing out of these circumstances a pattern, a design, a way of life which is uniquely her own.

Herald to Chaos

In Chapter X, Miss Roberts introduces a character, Luke Wimble, to make an explicit statement of the nature of Ellen's modern "heroism:"

"You're a bright shiny woman, Ellen Kent, and it's all I can do to keep my eyes offen you. The apple tree, it blooms with a little pink in the white and the peach is all pink. The dogwood is like a star in the forest and the redbud is a sunset against a hillside. Then there's honey and that's the fruit of the bee, the flower of the bee-gum, you might say. . . . They take the sweet outen the grass even, and even outen the mud. Some of it dark, the wild honey, and some strong and bitter, but all of it sweet, and it's the fruit of the bee. . . .

"You're worth all the balance put alongside each other. . . . You're worth all the balance and to spare. You got the very honey of life in your heart. Today I says to myself . . . I says, 'She's got the honey of life in her heart.' "

The fixed forces of life, here, as in the Homeric epic, are forces of relentless destruction; and, as in the classical epic, man's frontal assaults against these forces are futile romantic bursts of bravado. Ellen Chesser, like Odysseus, works within the frame of nature, bending to its will, partaking cooperatively of its strength, but always preserving in the security of her own identity the freedom, within nature's limitations, to create her own life in the best light of her own spirit. And thus, because of Miss Roberts' fundamental faith in the essential nobility of man, this stripped-to-the-bone "emblem of the common lot," Ellen Chesser, becomes unknowingly a representative of that which is best and most creative in man—the epic hero. Edward Garnett moves toward this perception in his review comment on *The Time of Man*: "The explanation of Miss Roberts' genius is not that she brings a new light into common folk's life, but she discovers the beauty that is there.

22

Moments of Union

Her spiritual vision has an irradiating power that harmonizes all the details . . . all are the living parts of the great mysterious whole."[4]

But before we leave the novel, we should examine it from the standpoint of form. Structurally, it is an almost perfect book, beginning with the slow lurching movements of a wagon on the road, its outer action proceeding as a series of episodes, paralleled always by the periodic thrusts and consolidations of Ellen's inner development, and ending with the same slow movement into the continuing distance with which it began. However, although the inner and outer action roughly parallel each other, they also establish a strong tension in contrast. The thrusts and consolidations of Ellen Chesser's cumulative growth are punctuated with moments of intense identification—as in her fierce realization by Judge Gowan's tombstone that she is "a-liven" and therefore incomparably superior to the dead judge. In a scene like this one, the march of the narrative ceases abruptly, and the lyrical emotion of the instant of comprehension absorbs the preceding events into a new harmony—a new attainment of form. Miss Roberts herself implies this kind of intention in the following note on the novel: "Some critic of *The Time of Man* said that it had probably grown up as a vine, bitter-sweet, a little and a little more. This minute growing, yes, but each minute (if you care) burst of life would come with a lyric fan-opening leap of words." She also left among her papers her own structural index to the novel:

I   A Genesis. She comes into the land. But the land
     rejects her. She remembers Eden (Tessie)
II   She grows into the land, takes soil or root. Life
     tries her, lapses in loveliness—in the not-lover Trent.
III Expands with all the land.

IV   The first blossoming.
V   Withdrawal—and sinking back into the earth.
VI   Flowering out of stone.

It can easily be seen that this analysis conforms to the chapter structure through the first four chapters of the novel. Chapters V, VI, and VII compose her fifth division, and Chapters VIII, IX, and X make up the "Flowering out of stone." The structure, as a whole, is thus designed to portray the developmental pattern of any man, and also of Miss Roberts' heroic everyman, for as Miss Roberts further suggests, the design of the novel reduces Ellen Chesser to the symbol of man as naked spirit fronting the most essential forces of life:

The design moves downward toward a nadir, step by step, to a sort of bottomless pit of woe. . . . The book is an outcry. Man, poor creature, loves his ease, his easy religions, his well-filled stomach, his nice prides in little things. He builds a pretty immortality for himself by way of the pageant enacted by the undertaker. He refuses to look closely at what he does not want to see. Insofar as he knows only exquisite spiritual sorrows he has not yet begun to suffer and has not yet begun to live.

Some critics feel that because the material of *The Time of Man* is selected largely from the underprivileged areas of American life, the novel should therefore be evaluated as a realistic "documentary" novel or a social-protest novel. They may left-handedly praise the novel as an attempt to show the sordid realities of life without making them completely sordid, or they may mildly shrug their shoulders over Miss Roberts' "pessimism."[5] It seems to me that this is somewhat like admiring the Iliad for its verisimilitude or its indignant exposé of the brutality of war. Miss Roberts' own defense, on this score, is adequate: "It could never be an analysis of society or

Moments of Union

of a social stratum because it keeps starkly within one consciousness, and that one being not an analytical or a 'conscious' consciousness." The last phrase in the preceding passage pinpoints, for me, one significant limitation of *The Time of Man*. We have seen that Ellen Chesser can symbolize the fundamental humanness of man—that quality which can create meaningful life out of the very rocks and roots of experience; but is she an adequate symbol for articulate, "conscious" twentieth-century humanity? In other words, granting the symbolic effectiveness of Ellen Chesser's contemporary Odyssey along the rut path subsistence level, we must still wonder whether there is not too much of a gap between the experience levels of the novel and the ordinary reader to allow participative identification between reader and protagonist.

However, this limitation ought not to divert attention from the real achievement of the novel. It is precisely because *The Time of Man* is not doctrinaire realism, but realism infused with poetry, that Ellen Chesser's creative struggle through life is capable of exalting and ennobling life itself. Her very "unconsciousness" serves to implicate her profoundly in the unending process of nature, while, at the same time, it makes her partial victory all the more impressive because it is so "natural." Miss Roberts' firm faith in the potency of the human spirit forms Ellen Chesser out of the earth and raises her far above the earth, even as she remains at one with it.[6]

MY HEART AND MY FLESH (1927): *Death and Resurrection*

MISS ROBERTS BEGAN thinking of her second novel as early as 1923, while she was engrossed in the writing of *The Time of Man*. Finishing *The Time of Man* in February, 1926, she set immediately to the writing of *My Heart and My Flesh*, and completed it a year and a half later. Of this second novel she wrote: "The method was a steady taking away until there was nothing left but the bare breath of the throat and the simplified spirit. . . . Out of the icy waters of the frozen pond . . . she experienced a resurrection. Spirit asserted itself over the necessities of death." She evidently thought of *The Time of Man* and *My Heart and My Flesh* as anti-theses during the period of the writing. She referred to the "process of accretion" in the former novel and the "continual subtraction" in the latter, going on to say: "Perhaps it is pleasanter to identify oneself with addition than with subtraction. As mathematics, the two processes are of equal value for art."

Miss Roberts' evident design was to present Theodosia Bell at the beginning of the novel as one of those fortunates on whom all opportunities have been bestowed with a lavish hand: wealth, family position, social prestige, education, musical talent; and then, by the process of "continual subtraction," to shear away, one by one, these cultural appurtenances until the naked soul is laid bare to the bone. And then, for Miss Roberts, the human spirit will assert itself by the faith drawn from its own soul, to ascend laboriously from

26

Moments of Union

the depths into life. The plan was an ambitious one, not made more workable by the characteristic subjective techniques which Miss Roberts used. The main difficulty she faced was that of avoiding sentimentality, on the one hand, and unintelligibility, on the other. An oversimplified handling of such material could easily dissolve into syrup, and sentimentality seems to have been one of Miss Roberts' chief horrors. On the other hand, to render in full the subtle complexities of the situation from within was to take the very real risk of sacrificing lucidity and confusing the reader past endurance.

Miss Roberts attempted to circumvent this latter danger by introducing the action with a long Prologue, narrated through the mind of Luce Jarvis, a neighborhood contemporary of Theodosia Bell. Miss Roberts explains this device as follows:

The mind here to be entered is the mind of the woman, Theodosia. The process begins with a knower, an observer, Luce, a sensitive onlooker. The narrative moves slowly into Theodosia's mind, beginning in the mind of Luce, seeing Theodosia first from the outside, moving more closely and intimately into her experience until it becomes identical with her consciousness. By this process I hope to be able to establish a spirit the more accurately and to present it with a movement which will approximate something lifelike.

The prologue is a phantasy. It begins in the mind of Luce, but it moves forward and backward in time and presents the background for what is to follow.

The Prologue, which fills thirty-three printed pages and is forcibly reminiscent of Marcel Proust's "Overture" in *Remembrance of Things Past*, contains some of Miss Roberts' finest writing. The girl Luce Jarvis has a sensitivity and an

27

alertness of impression even more acute than that of Ellen Chesser. Her mind weaves up and down the streets of Anneville, meeting all the major characters of the novel, Anthony, Horace, Charlotte, and Theodosia Bell, Stiggins, Ross, and even, with an exalted leap over miles, Caleb Burns. She gathers and records her impressions of dancing class, Sundays at church, and schooldays at the Seminary with a poetic charm and accuracy which establishes her character securely in the mind of the reader. For example, here is her impression of education:

> The song, all singing together, would roll out in a great shaking throb of noise and pain that beat upon sensitive ears and passed inward to become a pleasure, under the noise running the music.
>
> > Land where our fathers died,
> > Land where the Pilgrims pried, . . .
>
> Beyond the lessons of the books and the precepts of the teachers the young moved in the great flow of the body of human knowledge, learning slowly from one another. The fruit of knowledge passed downward perpetually from the older groups, becoming more grotesque as it descended beyond the reach of its accompanying emotions. The bulging piano legs on the chapel platform were with child, pregnant. The Pilgrims were thought of as a prying lot; they were heard of around Thanksgiving Day. A child had once designated his navel as his birthplace. . . . Word of it was passed about in a whisper; it was doubtless true; there was such a word; it could be found in the spelling book. In the assembly a child looked hard at the pregnant piano leg, trying to distinguish a mark upon it. Another day, and the mark was there, the birthplace.

But more importantly, Luce is presented as a seeker, a searcher into the underlying reality of appearances; her character and her function are suggested by her name. She is not

28

satisfied with the seeming aspect of things, and although she lacks the maturity to seek into the depths of being, she habitually attempts to. In a remarkable passage of sustained intensity, she tries to discover the "something within" Charlotte Bell, "searching down through blood and veins, liver and lights, smelt and kidney." She knows about Horace Bell's alliances with Tennie Burden and Dolly Brown, and she feels a compassion which she cannot understand for Stiggins, the halfwit stableboy son of Horace Bell. Through the use of juxtaposition, innuendo, and ominous overtones, the development of the story is confusedly foreshadowed: the pride of Theodosia, the decline of the Bells, the miscegenation theme, and even the regeneration of Theodosia.

One of the finest achievements of the Prologue is Luce's creation of the city of Mome, an imaginative world superimposed on the village of Anneville, which becomes an expansive symbol of life's possibilities and limitations as lyrically perceived by Miss Roberts through Luce. We have already observed in *The Time of Man* Ellen Chesser's deeplying dream of a vague idyllic security—a dream which functions to strengthen her spirit for the stresses of everyday life, even as it gives her a standard with which to meet and transform these stresses.[1] Mome (perhaps a portmanteau combination of "my home") is imaginatively projected out of the materials of Anneville. On its first level of creation, it is the naive wish fulfillment of a sensitive adolescent; it is everything that Anneville is not. It is large, modern, and romantically exciting:

There, in Mome, all the lights were electric, and there was one great light over all the place, a high great light like a sun. . . . It made a great sheet of light that spread over Mome as a sunset would spread over a hill. But there were dark alleyways for all

29

that, and dark doorways, and at the thought deep wells of feeling would pool up in one's chest, dark roadways and deep doorways and dark lanes where wheels had cut deep tracks.

In Mome there was nothing commonplace and dreary. There time never waited upon a fly-blown afternoon. Quick sayings flashed on the lips of men there, true finalities or bright quips—jests with the sudden tilt of quicksilver.

However, toward the end of the Prologue, the imaginary city has become far more significant than a childish daydream. It has severed its ties to any real or simulated place, it has become pure symbol, an unfettered vision of order and value: "Mome is disposed now, it is not a place now, is an actual substance as it was in the beginning, is become entirely what it always was. It has lost its delusion. No one ever called it now by a name."

Dependent originally for its existence on the imagination of Luce, it becomes a direct expression of the frame of reality through which the novel will move: "It is the four-arc'd clock of the seasons ticking its tick-tock around the year, and it is the mid-winter spring song of the joree bird, the Carolina wren, when he tee-teedle tee-teedle tee-deets on a high bare bough on a bright morning in January, spring not being here, not being there, not being anywhere." It partakes thus of the regular succession of the seasons, the continual flux of nature and the things which inhabit nature. In the swift poetic image of the Carolina wren, Miss Roberts implies both the beauty and the sadness of animate life within a limiting frame of forces.

It is the will to say, the power never being sufficient, the reach toward the last word—less than word, half-word, quarter-word, minimum of a word—that shrinks more inwardly and farthest toward its center when it is supplicated, that cries back, "Come,"

Moments of Union

or "Here, here I am," when it is unsought. It is the act of looking when the mirror of the earth looks back into a creature, back into quickened nerves and raw sensitive feelers that run to the ends of a town, gray and white threads, living threads, knotted into a net and contrived to catch and to hold pleasure and pain, chiefly to hold pain.

And here the relationship of the living growing searching human being to the object of his search is vividly suggested —the need, something not of the will, but of the very nature of life itself, to discover the basic fact of life which lies secretive, but alluring like the Sirens of myth, at the very center of being. The passage is extremely elusive, but its general feeling is communicated, and the note of pain which pervades the entire novel is here explicitly sounded. "It is the beauty of the thing itself welling up within itself continually in a constant rebirth, a resurrection. At any point it partakes of the whole nature of itself—like an onion." This is certainly clear enough; the continual growth, the harmony, and the overriding beauty expressed in a union, which points to the main theme of the novel: death and rebirth.

"It is nobody's useless old cat, having been stoned three times to death and left by boys in a tin-can heap at the bottom of a gully in Dee Young's pasture, arising, one eye hanging by a thread, to cry "meauw" on a woman's kitchen doorstep and to drink warm milk from a brown saucer." And here, another swift concretizing image expresses the fierce basic urge of life to live, to keep its tenacious hold on whatever it is that separates life from death.

This entire section on Mome is written in a rich poetic prose which soars far above the realistic frame of the novel. The metaphorical reach of the images is justified by the sensitive preparation of Luce's perceptions in the earlier part

31

of the Prologue, and Miss Roberts doubtless intended the creation of Mome as a kind of poetic statement of her ultimate concept of life which the Theodosia action of the book will strive to attain. I think, however, it fails for several reasons. First, the character of Luce, firmly established in the first pages of the novel, disappears out of the story. As we have seen, Miss Roberts hoped to merge Luce into Theodosia, keeping the two apart only so that Theodosia could be seen from without before the reader moves within her. However, Luce has so strongly gripped the reader's attention by the end of the Prologue, that Theodosia is much less interesting in comparison. And secondly, the rest of the novel is not organically attached to the Prologue (as is Proust's), so that this section gives the effect of being obtrusive and superfluous.

Miss Roberts could not have been insensitive to this structural discord, and it is possible that there are two explanations for her inclusion of the Prologue, other than the one already stated. First, she was at this time planning to incorporate *My Heart and My Flesh* into a linked-novel series to be called *The Books of Luce;*[2] with this consideration in mind, the disproportionate prominence of Luce would not be a weakness. And, perhaps more importantly, the creation of the Mome symbol might have weighed more heavily in her evaluation of the total effect of the novel than the resulting defect in structural organization. It is true that the Prologue is too weakly related to the rest of the novel, but it is also true that the total meaning of the novel would be much less without it. If my reasoning is correct, it is an understandable enough fault, and one which she was never to repeat.

At any rate, the narrative effect of the Prologue is reason-

Moments of Union

ably clear: Luce, "the knower," observes Theodosia from outside:

Her [Theodosia's] hair was brown with an over-tint of red that showed at the sides where the rolls were turned up to the light and showed again where the ends of the braid sprayed out beyond the ribbon below her shoulders and down her back. She spread a trail of herself down the platform as she went proudly first, the other girls walking on her steps, setting feet down where she guided, she leaving a comet-train of herself behind to be entered, walked into, known by the knower, the Chronicler.

Toward the end of the Prologue, Theodosia and Luce are supposed to merge into one consciousness, and the final section of the Prologue—the description of the Negroes laying water pipes through the village—is to set the scene at Anneville during Theodosia's childhood.

Chapter One opens with a more objective narrative tone, showing Theodosia as a vaguely unattractive, spoiled child, already too well convinced of her own superiority. Thus, in the scene when she visits the Negro quarters on the Singleton estate:

The little negroes would stare with strange dark faces, their mouths going up and down as they chewed at their fingers. Theodosia would watch every move they made, curious, following them, or she would go back to the quilt to watch the baby. She would watch their small dresses, their brown legs, their moving gestures, and she would ask them questions to pretend to an interest in their replies, but her pleasure was in her own sense of superiority and loathing, in a delicate nausea experienced when she knelt near the baby's quilt. . . . She knew the half-pleasant disgust felt for the young of another kind, a remote species. Their acts sent little stabs of joy over her, sickly stabs of pleasant contempt and pride.

And in spite of her pleasant abundance of childhood opportunities, there is something lacking in her complete enjoyment
of life:

Some abundance within herself would not let Theodosia
acquiesce completely to the hour, to any hour or to any experience
as being sufficient. . . . there were other beautiful things, other
best things. They eluded her, unnamed, receding down a long
vista into her inner sight. She recalled particular occasions when
the surrounding world had seemed good, a good place in which
to be. Admiring words from others, caresses, gifts, all the people
singing in the church—in the seed of each happening an insufficiency. There was never enough.

This "insufficiency of experience," which will haunt her
until the climactic episode of her self-realization, is the
gnawing force which impels her to seek for her spirit. For
although Theodosia has everything in the way of external
securities, she lacks the one thing which Ellen Chesser
possessed as her sole survival strength; this is, of course, an
unbidden embracing sense of self. Without this, she is
incapable of truly putting her universe in order; she can find
no ease or beauty within herself. She rushes frantically from
one thing to another—eager, dexterous and dissatisfied.

Theodosia went to school at the Seminary, or she practiced at
the fiddle half the day, exploring music without guidance. She
studied harmony at the school and assembled a small group there
to play quartets, her quick skill dominating. She grew tall in a
year. Her rounded breasts were up-tilted—two small graceful cups
—as if they would offer drink to some spirit of the air. She ran
swiftly from one thing to the next, the books in her grandfather's
cases, the fiddle, the games with the other girls.

When her sister Annie dies, Theodosia hears the funeral
hymn "as a bright myth having some celestial, candle-lit

meaning she could not understand." The mysteries of death and life have no roots in Theodosia's experience. She is unattached to nature, knowing nothing of its cycle of deaths and regenerations. Lacking a solid core of self-identity, she is evidently unable to feel any real emotion. We are told starkly that her mother, Charlotte Bell, "died one cold season when the town was numb and bewildered with the unaccustomed freezing." There is no comment about Theodosia.

This lack of a self-centered ordering mechanism in Theodosia probably explains the rapid pace at which the first chapter moves. Its many external events are not realized in a central core, and therefore there is very little real accumulation of personality. This flurry of meaningless activity is mirrored in the swift ejaculative effect of the style, as witness:

Anthony was palsied in his hands, but he would stop in his stroll along the path and beat the ground sharply with his cane, tapping on the bricks or on the boards under his feet. "Oh, tut!" he would say. Sometimes Theodosia would see him in his mantle of old age as he stepped uncertainly along, and a pang of pity, self-pity, fear, and apprehension would assail her. Or, seeing his shrunken form, his feet questioning the path for a place, she herself would walk there and she would see through her present self as through a swift glass, quickly adjusted for vision, as would say, "See, bent spine, eyes fixed, gestures squared at their turnings, the up-and-down jog of age." But her life ran upon itself eagerly and there were other things to see.

Missing here is the strongly participating vision with which the young Ellen Chesser characteristically views "the noise outside." Theodosia is a spectator, unable to measure "the life that ran upon itself so eagerly" for what it actually is: "a wind blowing in a mirror." Accordingly we find no spontaneous realizations of identity—no "Here I am's"—in her running consciousness. She perches like a timid elegant bird on the uncommitted margins of life, willing to see her pretty image reflected in the admiration of others, but incapable of generating any inner loveliness of her own.

Here, for example, is a description of Theodosia lying in bed in the early morning, snugly wrapped in her warm superficiality:

The warmth of the bed would shut about her in a matutinal caress as she sank into light half-slumber, as her mind fared here and yon in speculations and dreams, in plans and visions. The joy of friends would give her a pleasant sense of well-being, and her own warmed youthful blood would drowse and drown in its own relaxed languors. . . . Her speculating mind would run forward into the plans for the day, so many hours with the music, the fiddle, the harmony, the piano; or it would center briefly about some dress she was designing with the dressmaker or repairing for herself, and over this or through it would glide her floating senses as they drifted in the void. . . . The sound of the falling kindling would be heavy and remote. Between the separate sounds the spaces of quiet would be light with dreaming, with herself drowned in joy and myth, drooping in strong up-reaching fingers, Albert's hands, but over her and above like the light of some final dawn, radiant but self-contained and entire, identical with light negligent laughter, would float some essence that merged with Conway and with her happiness.

The accent of this passage is unmistakably passive rather than active. Theodosia is rendered in terms of "relaxed languors," "floating," "drifting," "drowsing" in "light negligent laughter." Comparing her with Ellen Chesser, we can readily see that in the inmost core of her being, Theodosia is dead, or at least unborn. Her life is realized in fragile evanescent meanings, comforted by a tenuous external security which the slightest gust of the weathers will rip aside. It is at this point that the "process of subtraction" begins, stripping away one by one the false masks beneath which Theodosia conceals her lack of self.

The first illusion to go is her treasured family respectability. She who had for so long assumed an automatic superiority in her family position discovers not only that she is poor, but also that she has two sisters and a brother in the long-loathed Negro community of Anneville. What had been an unquestioned source of identity—to be a Bell of Anneville—becomes a corrupt mockery. She turns toward Anthony Bell, her grandfather, searching him for some root meaning which will establish herself in relation to something absolute, dependable:

Her outer vision dulled by the fire and by weariness, her inner vision heightened, she began to divide her being, searching for some soul or spirit. Her search took her into her grandfather's being where it touched accurately to her own. He was old, withered, palsied, but he had life, a life, from first to last, she observed and the house was real for him and the people of the house, the pain of his sickness.

As she studies her grandfather, attempting to discover the secret strength that he owns—a strength which she now perceives to be nonexistent within her—she finds herself unconsciously becoming kind to him, gratuitously giving of herself to help him. The Theodosia who could not bear to have the slightest physical contact with anything foul or sick or alien comes to a point where she bathes the old man lovingly.

She loathed nothing that he might reveal and she looked at him searchingly. She remembered that his knowledge was gone or blurred; he could no longer lay his hand upon it; it was gone then;

his charm was gone. What, she questioned, did his spirit have to do with his knowledge, with his person, his courage, his putrefying flesh, his taste, his temper, his determination, his belief in herself? He wanted to be alive, secret, shut within himself. She tried to eliminate from herself all but that which they held in common and, the cancellations made, to identify something which one could describe as deathless, as indicative of a man. Her tenderness intervened, however, and she found that she had resolved to make him some light flannel caps to protect his head from the cold while he slept. She felt a holy sense of comfort when she went softly from his door.

This tenderness is probably her first large step toward redemption; this is her first unselfish act which, paradoxically, becomes her first experience in the long chain of experiences necessary to her self-discovery.

Meanwhile, even as her search for self continues, the process of subtraction accelerates. Albert Stiles, who had promised to marry her whether she was willing or not, deserts her.[3] And, more importantly, she learns that her hand is not broad enough to accomplish the fingering necessary to move into the outer reaches of musical experience, and her violin becomes an instrument of narcissistic self-pity instead of a way of self-discovery. She had been told that "music must come out of the soul," and she had been seized by a fervent passion for music: "I want to play the fiddle to the end of the earth. I want to go to the end of music and look over the edge at what's on the other side." Her physical limitations with the violin, however, are symbolic of the spiritual vacancy which marks her uncommittedness to life. Music can express, but it cannot create, the soul; Theodosia with her violin is in a twofold sense a dilettante, not an artist. That the music motif is significant in this novel can be seen in Miss Roberts' notation on Theodosia: "Why did she not

38

find the soul in music? (language of) approach but not soul itself."[4]

Conway Brooke, another tentative suitor, dies in the burning of his house, and this death gives Theodosia an opportunity to find a temporary security in a posthumous passion for his memory—a passion which cannot involve her in a real sharing relationship, because it occurred in another country, and besides, the wretch is dead:

As her memory grew more intense, dwelt upon, the intensity of her grief multiplied, gathered now into a passion for Conway, whom she was free to mourn and long for. She remembered every gesture and posture of his body, conned each one to bring it back to being, and focused about his jealousy, which had become precious now, and about his bitter, hurt replies, that fell the more poignantly in that they were surrounded by his lightness and carelessness. She was free to love him and to want him. Her hate of Albert inverted itself and became an intense passion for Conway.

In this assumed passion, her occupation becomes that of a shrine servitor; she has no friends; she has no love save that which she lives in the imagined past. She remains in her room, playing the violin, enjoying to the fullest that precious grief, about which Miss Roberts wrote: "Man, poor creature, loves . . . his nice prides in little things. . . . Insofar as he knows only exquisite spiritual sorrows he has not yet begun to suffer and has not yet begun to live."

She would speak to him [Conway] continually, commenting on each effort and each achievement, assuming him in mind as a companion. . . . Or, inarticulate before what she did, articulating only with the cry of the strings, she felt such rush of impulse as would say: Here in this succession of sound cries out a sorrow greater than our personal sorrows, the sorrow of the whole of man at finding himself in an earth addicted to time. As would say:

39

Herald to Chaos

Here in the adagio man spreads out the infinite tentacles of his multiform being, his personality, and lays, kind for kind, each sensitive feeler upon a like that protrudes from the Source. As would say: This theme, a pastoral from some central-European rolling plain, is ours as we sit in the heart of this land where the seasons rise and fall in waves, a melancholy procession, and men mark their time with their labor as they roll the soil over from year to year endlessly plowing. Conway was with her in these articulations, in the breath of her throat, in the beat of her right hand over the gut wires.

The irony of this passage makes the pomposity of Theodosia's sentiments (because they are so unrelated to her life experience) unmistakable.

However, this self-indulgent role of Theodosia's is short lived; rumor becomes bruited about that Minnie Harter, a young woman of the town, is bearing Conway's unborn child, and with this last illusion sheared away, Theodosia is forced once more to look truly within herself: "A suspicion grew in the arising confusion of her thought that her own posthumous passion for Conway had been identified with her lost hope of the fiddle, with her tenderness and self-love that had been shielding her limitation from inner examination and despair. . . . The shock of the argument opened new vistas down into the dark of her inner thought."

Chapter Four accelerates the pace of the descent into the tomb, and the tone of the prose moves up a pitch giving the effect of a steady, half-heard, unignorable shriek. Theodosia moves as in a dream, unable to find herself, but at the same time, protecting herself from the realization of reality. This is well delineated in a remarkable dream episode which occurs as Theodosia dozes in her vigil beside Anthony's bed. She dreams of the figure of a man, standing before a multitude of haggard women:

Moments of Union

He was one, one man, heroic in size, bursting with strength and life, made of flesh like a man. He stood erect, his limbs apart, in a lewd pose. He was naked. On his body were marks then; on his chest they began, as small warts sprinkled over his breast, but lower, on his upper abdomen, they were larger and were shaped like small teats. They became larger as they descended over his abdomen and became more alive, each one more living than the last. They were rigid with life and were pointed forward toward the women.

Her own self stood at her elbow. She turned quickly about, toward her self, and she knew a deep wish, an ardent prayer that her self had not seen this last. Her self had not seen, was watching the women as they were going far down the street. . . . Her self had not seen it. She was glad with a great thankful prayer.

The dream symbolizes, at least as one of its meanings, Theodosia's coupling of the basic life urge, the sexual drive, with something monstrously lewd—something to be hidden away from herself, lest she be soiled by the knowledge. This refusal to accept reality, or to look at it only in the hidden corners of her mind with prurient eyes, is unmistakable evidence of her closing herself off from the wellsprings of life.

We are thus not surprised that after Anthony's death and Horace's departure, leaving Theodosia alone in the great house piled up with debts, she moves to the very edges of insanity, seeking frantically to discover some external support on which she can lean her own emptiness. She goes to the Negro quarters, immersing herself in Americy and Stiggins' incestuous passion and Lethe's violent hatred. In the ugly violence of her sisters' and brother's lives, she finds something active which she can throw herself into, because she possesses nothing solid of her own:

In Lethe hate was apotheosized, a hungry god, ravenous, beside an altar waiting for food. Lethe's breath was fluted and

41

broken, timed to the beating of her heart, marked by regular sobs that were softly voiced now and then. Her eyes were beyond seeing, turned glassy with their own inner sight. . . . Theodosia pushed her chair near the table and bent one knee into it. . . . She stood over Lethe, leaning slightly forward, and her breath became hard, fluted with the beating of her own heart where anger began to arise and was timed to Lethe's panting breath.

For Theodosia, Lethe's unfaithful husband Ross is identified with Albert, whose body is "rich with blood and bulk" like the lewd figure of her dream, and she sucks Lethe's anger into herself, goading Lethe to murder, loathing these filthy savage creatures as dark extensions of her own being: "Theodosia felt her body slipping into the chair and leaning nearer. She wanted justice. She leaned close to Lethe's body, her hands on the edge of the table beside Lethe's hands. She was shut in a complete stillness and she was mingled with Lethe's anger and hate." On the following morning, Ross is dead at Lethe's hands, and Theodosia, her borrowed energy entirely spent, lies numb with fever.

Chapter Five contains some of the most remarkable writing that I know of in contemporary literature. The time-span is approximately eighteen months—eighteen months of a long gray convalescence, in which Theodosia moves to the very edge of suicide, halts, and begins her return to life. The setting and atmosphere are surrealistic; the house (the Singleton estate), the characters, Theodosia's state of mind, the wild dogs—all are blurred into indistinct but insistent shapes which howl at the fringes of the consciousness. The setting is thus a perfect allegorical projection of the hysteria which marks Theodosia's descent into the living veins of her soul. To show more clearly the profound derangement of Theodosia's inner being, as well as the arguments which lead her

Moments of Union

toward suicide, Miss Roberts employs a dialog which advances with surrealistic logic, alluding to the Bell family history, remembering fragments of disconnected poetry (Browning and Emerson), but more importantly, hammering at the unworthiness of Theodosia to live, if the universe is a moral one—charging her with murder, adultery, and dishonor of her parents. The arguments then shift their tack, holding the position that there is no meaning in life, that man is merely "a nervous system"; that if goodness had any significance, her sister Annie would never have died:

First Voice: I saw the picture of a man, a real speaking likeness. It was a ten-thousand-footed octopus. . . . A ten-thousand-footed serpent, every foot a feeler out to feel something.
Second Voice: A maw in the middle of it, the chief part, the chief part set in the middle, a hungry enlargement in the alimentary gut.
Third Voice: Another maw in the lower middle, the chiefest chief part, another hungry entrail, if you don't like the short word.
First Voice: A little knob, a very little knob on the top. I saw the true likeness. An infinite number of feelers running out all ways, shaped like a serpent, and a very little knob on the top.

To this Theodosia can only counter with the climactic scream of the novel: "Oh, God, I believe, and there's nothing to believe."

Finally, starved in both body and spirit to the last edge of endurance, Theodosia prepares herself for suicide in the frozen pond. And then her moment of revelation toward which the whole book has been building arrives:

At once a vivid appearance entered her mind, so brilliant and powerful that her consciousness was abashed. Larger than the world, more spacious than the universe, the new apparition spread through her members and tightened her hands so that they

43

knotted suddenly together. It tightened her spine until she sat erect. Her recognition settled to a word, groped with words, settled again about a word, some word, catching at words with a net. The word was vivid, was like a new flower in a sunny place, and unable to say it she knew it with a rush of thanksgiving that out-ran all her recognition of it. The word she could not say, could only approach with reaching tentacles of memory and thought erecting a joy throughout her senses. Her body spread widely and expanded to its former reach, and the earth came back, herself acutely aware of it. A pleasure that she still lived to participate in this recognition caught her throat with a deep sob. . . . The word let a happy substitute stand for itself, a delegate appearing clearly defined, a word experienced as a glow of pride in life and joy. "Tomorrow" was the utterance, clearly placed then. . . . This homely habitual fact had been the Arise-ye of her resurrection. "I'm still alive," she sang under her breath, "I'm alive. I'm alive." She leaned tensely near the hearth and spoke, or she smiled without speaking. Her eyes were dim with the new birth and the bloom of renascence slightly blurred her consciousness as yet. The loaned word grew more vivid, "Tomorrow," substituted now for the unsaid word that receded, its mission accomplished.

In this moment of self-recognition and assertion of the will to live the dissociated fragments of Theodosia's being are made whole and beautiful and electric with life.

As her new life begins, the pace of the novel slows to a more gentle, leisurely swing of cadences, approximating the pastoral regularity of the flow of the seasons. Theodosia merges into the life of the country, serving as teacher in a rural school. She learns to accept reality as a growing organism, unafraid now to accept any of its aspects. Thus, when she finds her blackboard covered with obscenities, she is not fearful of evaluating them in proportion to the whole pattern of life:

Moments of Union

She erased the words, seeing them, unafraid of them. They named the excretions of the body and the acts of excretion, she observed. If one is to name the discharges of the body, he should name them all, she thought, looking at the last of the words as she erased. Name them all, slighting none. Among these words should be written the omitted word, a true juice of the human frame, *tear*. Spelled with four letters, as were the other words, she ruminated, belonging with the others entirely. Let the boy, whoever he was . . . write the last word; he would write it in time, this supreme juice from the body of man, the point where he stands above himself, where he outdoes the cattle.

And when Caleb Burns offers her his love, she finds that her new life has grown over, has absorbed, has amalgamated the old life into itself, and she can go forth to her lover clean and whole:

Then she remembered hell. A clear sharp memory, acutely realized, the more acutely realized in that it fell in this moment of pleasure. Self appeared, saturated with memory-realization, herself subtracted from the earth and elevated to a pinnacle of searching, her body hungering, seeing itself slipping into decay. All the disconnections operating, everything was lost then but Frank. Frank in her hands and her fingers, her shoulders, her name, her sight, her sleep. Pure and excruciating distress shook her as if it were a chill and she called to her grandfather, Anthony Bell, but when she was more quiet again, the memory receding, she called in mind the newer name.

This remarkable book is extremely difficult to evaluate. Its relative lack of popularity is probably adequately explained by the "unpleasantness" of its subject matter, as Professor Wagenknecht has pointed out.[5] Glenway Wescott lists it as his favorite of all Miss Roberts' novels,[6] and J. Donald Adams writes: "It is a novel which has at times an almost terrifying power; dealing with a somewhat Faulknerian theme, it reduces Faulkner to melodramatic claptrap."[7] Kenneth Burke, on the other hand, writes: "In *My Heart and My Flesh*, we remain unmoved by the heroine's aberations, which are conveyed less by psychological disclosure than by tricks of presentation."[8] It is difficult to imagine how else a novelist can disclose character except by tricks of presentation, but I suppose Burke is referring to the "Voices" in Chapter Five. Janney's criticism of the novel strikes me as more fruitful; he recognizes the power of the theme, but finds Theodosia too "thin" a character to sustain the weight of meaning which the novel lays on her.[9] Miss Roberts herself seems to have been comparably dissatisfied with the character of Theodosia. In her papers there is this notation:

Do I write about Theodosia less lovingly than I did of Ellen? If so why is this. . . .
Ellen is and was for me life itself. Have I less sympathy for Theodosia? Why? What is she? How does she relate to life?
She is a wandering spirit, a lost thing.
Why is she lost more than Ellen is?
She is lost through a partial consciousness which leads her to set up standards and anti-standards. Ellen is not lost because she belongs to the earth itself, to the swing of the tides . . . of the seasons.

Whether or not Miss Roberts' lack of sympathy for Theodosia is the cause, I think it is true that the characterization exerts less of a grip on the reader's empathies than it might conceivably have done. A comparison with one of the great archetypal resurrection figures in literature, King Lear, will make manifest the difference. Lear, going through the same kind of subtraction process to find himself, to incorporate himself into the common membership of mankind, never loses his firm grasp on the reader's affections. Theodosia, on the other hand, stands apart from the reader too long; and, therefore, her torturous trials affect him more as a case history than as a moving literary experience. But granting the slight discord of structural form, allowing for the argument that Theodosia's character tends to alienate the reader, granting even that the subordinate characters (with the possible exception of Anthony Bell) are incompletely realized—still the novel records an achievement which is rare in contemporary American literature. It probes with an awesome honesty into the darkest areas of the human soul, the area where morality and order have their genesis. And without sentimentality it enfleshes the psalmist's cry: "My heart and my flesh crieth out for the living God"; and it answers this cry.

My Heart and My Flesh is a novel that Miss Roberts probably was forced to write, after writing *The Time of Man.* As we have noted, *The Time of Man* suggested questions which could not be answered within its symbolic plan; *My Heart and My Flesh* answers these questions. What about the twentieth-century man not on the primitive subsistence level? What about the human being with the advantages of education and culture? Where will he find his morality, his order, his significance in life? These questions we asked, and *My Heart and My Flesh* pointed for answer to the same place. "Life is from within." The "living God" is within; seek there and ye shall find.

CHAPTER THREE

The Outlying Spaces

THE GREAT MEADOW (1930): Genesis and Exodus

ALTHOUGH *The Great Meadow* was Miss Roberts' fourth novel in order of publication, it has been reported that she first conceived of the book as far back as 1915, before she went to Chicago.[1] It certainly seems to be the one of all her novels which allowed her to move most freely among the materials and techniques she knew best. The background is the late eighteenth-century settlement of Kentucky, and the people are such as she imagined her own pioneer ancestors to be. Further, the chronicle of a people's conquest of the wilderness lends itself to a symbolic mergence with one of her major themes—the individual's creation of order out of the chaos of sensations. And Miss Roberts' concept of communality, nurtured on the ideals of Jeffersonian democracy, could here find illustration in the people's creation of a national life—the social level of meaning which parallels symbolically the life-creating activities of the book's heroine, Diony. The result, *The Great Meadow,* has been the most highly regarded of all Miss Roberts' novels.[2]

In *The Time of Man* we noted that the structural rhythm of that novel was drawn from the unending struggle of man, each day fighting a new battle, retiring at nightfall stronger inwardly with the fruits of the day's victory, but forced to face another battle on the morrow. We saw that the heroic qualities of man, for Miss Roberts, lay in the dignity and courage and self-faith with which man faced his battles. In *My Heart and My Flesh* the same onward-going ebb-and-flow rhythm was applied to Theodosia's agonizing descent into herself in order to discover that self, followed by the slow blossoming of the self made whole and realized. The same rhythm, but this time applied to the spiritual death and rebirth of the central character, Ellen's story having been one of continuing growth.

In *The Great Meadow* there are two major movements, the cumulative growth of Diony as she imposes order on the world within her, and the westward march of the colonies creating order and civilization in the untamed wilderness. Both movements are characterized symbolically in the novel with images of birth and begetting—variations, as we can see, of this same undulating flux which inches forward toward an eternally receding goal. The two movements do not operate completely on parallel planes, however; they interact symbolically and sometimes fuse. At times Diony becomes a brooding mother symbol of America; and the American experience of frontier expansion becomes a symbol of the individual's lonely struggle with the elements beyond his soul.

Herald to Chaos

The novel opens with Diony, sixteen years old, in the home of her father in Albemarle County, Virginia. The year is 1774. From her father's family, Diony has the heritage of the tidewater gentry; her mother was a Pennsylvania Methodist; hence Diony is born with the mixture of blood and backgrounds which Miss Roberts felt to be representative of those late eighteenth-century pioneers who settled Kentucky.

I saw these people coming over the Trace, some of them coming early when there were hundreds of miles of scarcely broken forests to be passed. The drama was brief, but it was full and picturesque. I thought it would be an excellent labor if one might gather all these threads, these elements, into one strand, if one might draw these strains into one person and bring this person over the Trace and through the Gateway in one symbolic journey.

Tidewater gentry, scholarship, pagan lore, English communicants, and Catholics, wealth and ease, family pride, these are met by sturdy races of tradesmen and farmers, Methodists—most despised sect of the century—Puritanic, Quaker, provident, holy, aggressive, of great bodily vigor and a sturdy beauty. They were on fire with their own flame. These elements gathered into the parents of this woman, Diony. Perhaps the reader will discover something more. The dramatic passage, the gateway, the Wall, could not be ignored.

Five Oaks, the Hall homestead, is on the outer fringes of the frontier, geographically situated at the point where order and chaos impinge on one another: "Thus the tilled land and the unbroken forests touched their parts about Diony." But not only is Diony at the geographical juncture of chaos and order; within her own sixteen-year-old experience are conjoined the wilderness and civilization. Through her father's old letters and his reminiscent talk, she is able to recreate the life of the tidewater in her memory so vividly that it becomes a real experience for her, and she is able to visualize the life of brocaded gowns and powdered pompadours for her younger sister, Betty. Her early exposure to Berkeley has made her highly sensitive to the existence of unordered infinity, of chaos unsubdued by mind; and Sallie Tolliver, a woman on whom the wilderness has laid its inexorable hand, moves like a stricken wraith through the Hall household. Significantly, Miss Roberts compares Diony with Ellen Chesser: "Ellen is more a creature of the ground. Diony is a creature of the mind, moving always more inwardly." *The Time of Man* opened with Ellen Chesser spontaneously asserting her identity by writing her name in the air with her finger; *The Great Meadow* opens with Diony introspectively deducing the existence of the world itself from her own self-awareness: "The world reached straight then, into infinity, laid out beyond the level of herself in a far-going horizontal, although report said of it that it bent to a round and made a globe. She was aware of infinity outward going and never returning. 'I, Diony,' she said."

In *The Time of Man*, the narrative point of view was so thoroughly restricted to the consciousness of Ellen Chesser (who was not, as Miss Roberts pointed out, an "analytical" creature), that hers was the only consciousness that was realized. In that novel, this was not at all a fault; it was in fact a tour de force. In *My Heart and My Flesh*, however, we noted that the characters subordinate to Theodosia Bell were too shadowy to convince; because of the surrealistic pitch of the novel, this was not as serious a flaw as it might have been, but it seemed to limit Miss Roberts to the creation of one character per novel. Here, in *The Great Meadow*, there is a distinct advance in the rendering of subordinate characters—an advance facilitated largely by the greater lucidity

51

of Diony's perceptions of human contacts, and a more sophisticated employment of dialog to reveal character. Such subordinate characters as Thomas and Betty Hall, Berk and Elvira Jarvis, and Daniel Boone emerge in sharper outline than we might have expected, without a corresponding loss in the subjective perceptions of the main character.

Moreover, because Diony is a "creature of the mind," she is consciously motivated to impose form on chaos: "Her thought leaped then beyond articulation and settled to a vast passion of mental desire. Oh, to create rivers by knowing rivers, to move outward through the extended infinite plane until it assumed roundness. Oh, to make a world out of chaos." This conscious desire to subdue the infinities of chaos into finite knowable order makes Diony a fitting symbol for the American frontier experience; that is, she can be both pioneer and pioneering.

Reports of the "promise land" which lies beyond almost inaccessible mountains, this "well-nigh sort of Eden . . . Caintuck," are brought into the Hall household. The grandeur of the vast, rich-flowing caneland, the seven beautiful rivers with the wonderful names that trill on the tongue, and the legendary woodcock with the ivory beak, create an image of Paradise: "Rich cane. Trees all in blowth in the spring o'-the year. Like paradise it is, so beautiful and good." The way was long and the ordeal of settlement beset with dangers that the mind could not even imagine. But once the unknown is defined and circumscribed by the known, it exerts a powerful attraction on the human spirit, and this insatiable urge to extend experience is integral to Miss Roberts' concept of human growth.

The frontiersmen in Albemarle County react instinctively to the challenge of the unsubdued West. Man cannot forage into the unknown without himself being changed, but because man has instinctive faith in the virtue of knowledge—Miss Roberts believed—he assumes that this change will be for the better. To experience suffering, to impart a design on that which is without design, in short, to "know" in the dynamic, cumulative, creative sense which Miss Roberts pours into this all-important verb, is the one vital "good" in human life. Thus the settlement of the original thirteen colonies, the belief of the early Puritans in their divine commission to create a "New Jerusalem" in the wilderness, the establishment of a Federal Republic of the United States of America, are, for Miss Roberts, almost poems—group manifestations of the same urge that impels Diony "to create rivers by knowing rivers. . . . Oh, to make a world out of chaos." And thus, as the Halls sit by their fireside in the ordered security of Five Oaks, they dream of the untouched land beyond the mountains: "Such a country would breed up a race of heroes, men built and knitted together to endure."

One further element should be added here. Diony is not only self-conscious—"a creature of the mind"—but she is also vaguely aware of her destiny as a symbol:

Diony knew what name she bore, knew that Dione was a great goddess, taking rank with Rhea, and that she was the mother of Venus by Jupiter, in the lore of Homer, an older report than that of the legendary birth through the foam of the sea. She knew that Dione was one of the Titan sisters, the Titans being earthmen, children of Uranus and Terra. . . . She could scarcely piece the truths together to make them yield a thread of a story, but she held all in a chaotic sense of grandeur, being grateful for a name of such dignity.

Uranus and Gaea conquered Chaos in their symbolic wedding which parallels the creation of the universe. Diony, then, in rough parallelism, stands for man subduing nature. Or, as Miss Roberts points out in her notes: "Nature arising above the infinitives of matter, above the indefinite and everlasting fixity of matter with its 'chemistry.' Man then arising above Nature."

Miss Roberts, thus, very early in the novel, suggests quite explicitly the symbolic direction which the novel will take. So Diony rejects the suitor who brings a promise of elegance and a secure future:

> Diony had a picture of herself sitting at a piece of musical furniture and she felt her fingers tripping lightly over the little white keys, making a tinkle to accompany her song. The tunes tingled in her arms and in her shoulders, wanting an outlet by way of her hands, and she went swiftly in mind down into the lower country with this Nathaniel Barlow to sit there on elegant chairs and bow and curtsey at strange doorways, herself settled, at home there, on land she owned for her own home. But she let him pass finally, and let the low countries be diffused, taking their spinets into fogs of unknown ways.

And she accepts the proposal of Berk Jarvis to come with him to Harrodstown, the new settlement at the end of Boone's Wilderness Road: "They would go to the country behind the mountains and start a new world there, he said." Spasmodic reports of fighting in Boston, the sitting of the Continental Congress, and the signing of the Declaration of Independence sift gradually into Five Oaks, infusing Berk's "to start a new world" with a continental significance.

As the preparations for the movement westward are completed and the marriage takes place, Thomas Hall acts as chorus, interpreting the dramatic activity at Five Oaks in relation to the immutable principles of life:

The Outlying Spaces

Men, he said, were the mouths of the earth, and through them the earth spoke in the general; but a man, in the particular instance, might understand and interpret and might see the signs put forth by the Author and Designer to reveal what lay under the outer show of properties and kinds. He told of one wonder after another, of deviations from the natural law, but he told again of how the kept law is a greater marvel than the deflected law, and how it, by its sufferance of the other, continually reveals a purpose beyond the knowledge of men. He would not stand in Diony's way, he said. . . .

"For such a length of time as it staggers the mind to contemplate, Man has been marching outward. . . . Civilized Man is forever spreading more widely over the earth, historic Man bringing such men as have no history to humble themselves and learn their lesson. It's a strong mark of the hidden purposes of the Author of all things. . . . It will never be said of me I hindered Diony."

The law of nature, as Thomas Hall understands it, is that of continual cumulative progress through constant rebirths; the daughter must leave the father, childhood must give way to maturity, naissance must be followed by renaissance. And returning us to the theme of *The Time of Man*, Thomas Hall intones the first verses of the *Aeneid*:

His voice breaking from the Latin chant would concede known meanings to all that he had sung, as "I sing of arms and the hero who, fate driven, first came from the shores of Troy to Italy and the Lavinian coast, he, *vi superum*, by the power of the gods, much tossed about, *multum jactatus*, much tossed about on land and sea."

The journey of Diony is thus invested with the significance of that other journey to found a nation, and the symbolic reach of the action ascends into the epic plane.

The marriage ceremony itself, performed under Methodist

auspices in a county where only Church of England marriages were legal before the Declaration of Independence, is an emblem of defiance to the old way and a revolutionary adoption of the new, as the murmurs of dissatisfaction among the wedding guests testify:

"Hit's a wilderness marriage. Let be." One or two spoke.
"Married for the wilderness."
"Don't trouble their souls with doubt."
"It's a miracle; the old law come back."
"Married fit for the wilderness."
"Without law, but no matter."
"Quiet! A new day. No matter."
"Amen, amen, amen."

And thus, Diony, carrying the heritage of all her forebears, yearning to create something new of her own, moves forward into the unknown:

Suddenly, in the tinkling of the bells, she knew herself as the daughter of many, going back through Polly Brook through the Shenandoah Valley and the Pennsylvania clearings and roadways to England, Methodists and Quakers, small farmers and weavers, going back through Thomas Hall to tidewater farmers and owners of land. In herself then an infinity of hopes welled up, vague desires and holy passions for some better place, infinite regrets and rending farewells mingled and lost in the bended inner tinkle and clatter. These remembrances were put into her own flesh as a passion, as if she remembered all her origins, and remembered every sensation her forebears had known.

The travail of the five-hundred-mile trek from Five Oaks to Fort Harrod—the long journey along the valley of the Shenandoah, the crossing of the New River at Inglis Ferry, the repeated crossings of the Holston and the Clinch rivers, the laborious march over Powell Mountain—culminates sym-

56

The Outlying Spaces

bolically not in the arrival at Fort Harrod but in the dramatic passage through the gap in the great cliff barrier which guards Kentucky from the outside world. The land itself is portrayed in the act of giving birth to a new people; the long period of gestation, the laborious passage through the mountains, and the miraculous ejection of new life are implicit in the description of the long journey:

Together, men and women, they went slowly forward, the men to the fore, the man's strength being in the thrust, the drive, in action, the woman's lateral, in the plane, enduring, inactive but constant. They marched forward, taking a new world for themselves, possessing themselves of it by the power of their courage, their order, and their endurance.

The whole line . . . were small beings, contrived for endurance, and they crept through the earth and burrowed through overgrown gulches. They were small gaunt creatures, thrusting forward, their sinews able to thrust again even after weariness had settled over them.

And when the marchers near Harrod's fort, they have the glow and wonder of the newborn upon them; indeed, the connotations of the birth are somewhat Wordsworthian:

The path emerged from the hills and came out onto the great fertile plateau where the rolling forests lay as a giant mantle over the earth. . . . They went plodding down under noble trees, their limbs crooked to the weariness of going and their sinews strained, their gaunt frames beating forward. Diony could now remember what lay far behind. Over her thought flowed continually a freshness as if the world were new-born. . . .
Around them stretched the delirium of a fine land, level expanses delicately tilted to fine curves. . . .
"What do we want here? What did we come for?" She was shaken with delight and wonder.

And thus, through a remarkable interfusion of symbolism (the coupling of the Declaration of Independence with this migration "to start a new world"), the birth of a nation and the birth out of a nation become dramatically realized at one and the same time.[3]

In the significant meeting between Diony and Daniel Boone, when Diony thanks Boone for making the road through the wilderness over which she has traveled, Boone's answer reasserts Miss Roberts' belief in the creative base of individual experience: " 'You're right welcome to it,' Boone said. 'If I marked out the way, you had to go it with your two feet, and so the road's yours too for the trouble you took to walk it. And the danger was yours whilst you went the way.' " Thus the pilgrimage of man is everyman's, and no matter how many have gone before, the path is always new, dangerous, and self-created. The further conversation between Diony and Boone illuminates the contrast between the two kinds of strength which human beings possess: "the man's strength being in the thrust, the drive, in action, the woman's lateral, in the plane, enduring, inactive but constant." Diony suggests to Boone that there are many places in Kentucky where "a body could get lost in and never find himself again." Boone's reply is significant: " 'I don't reckon I'd get lost in e'er one. Not to say lost. I never was lost. I was bewildered right bad once for as much as a week, but not lost. I never felt lost the whole enduren time.' " Later Diony reflects on this answer:

[She] felt the breadth of the out-reaching land as she had had report of it from one and another, as if it had been there beside her at the gate, as if it had come in the flesh to breathe and smile, to speak to her. "Never lost, not once the whole enduren time," she said, smiling. "It's curious." She walked three steps beyond the gate and looked at the four parts of the sky to try to place herself rightly under it, to set the winds to rights and to feel secure above the green of the earth. "I'm not the Boone kind," she said. "I never was. . . . I'd be more at home somewheres else . . . I don't know where."

The distinction is an important one for Miss Roberts' concept of ordering chaos; the one strength, the Boone strength, is that which leaps outward into the unknown, blazing the pioneer trail into the wilderness without substantially altering the wilderness. The Diony kind of strength, on the other hand, is that which follows the trail after it is blazed, setting things in order, establishing a routine and a familiarity in the areas barely wrested out of the grip of chaos. This strength Miss Roberts generally thinks of as a female strength; the first is more closely associated with the physical, but the second is mental.[4] The strengths are, of course, complementary, and each is an application of the "life is from within" principle.

Miss Roberts evidently became aware that the kind of intuitive ordering of experience which we saw so beautifully illustrated in *The Time of Man* was not a sufficient concept to explain the workings of social groups; accordingly, we see her supplying a complementary kind of idea to encompass all the activities by which progress is made. Under the Boone kind of man, we can include the explorer, the brilliant theorist, the visionary artist, and similar people who push out the frontiers of human knowledge; the Diony kind then follows the path streaked erratically on the outermost edge of the horizon, absorbing and ordering the new territory into the settled possession of mankind. Some journal notations of Miss Roberts' will substantiate this view:

Diony represents ordered life and the processes of the mind, the mind life. She is not of the Boone kind. She feels lost in an indefinite universe. She wants ordered ways. She wants beauty and dignity and ceremony and the reasons of all things.

Boone represents the indefinite earth, the outside of chaos, but he is an apostle to chaos to prepare it for man's order.

In Boone alone we had a symbol of man leaping apart from men, thrusting forward to a lonely and hazardous freedom among the natural and chaotic things of the unmapped earth.

In Boone man inserted himself into the grass. Went a little way with the grass to overcome the grass—Bold Chevalier.

With the impetus of this additional concept, the symbolic connotations of the novel expand to a higher, more universal plane, and we find that *The Great Meadow* is at once a chronicle of Diony's ever-increasing personality, a narrative which catches the distilled meaning of the American experience, and a symbolic affirmation and analysis of the progress of mankind.

This becomes explicit in the long dream of a "civil society" which Diony projects, sitting alone in a cabin in Fort Harrod in 1778. She realizes that her "new birth" is merely one of endless births which she must undergo in her insistence to remain alive—that "she was a beginning before the beginning."[5] And in the implications of the dream, we see that she realizes that mankind, striving to advance into uncharted areas, must likewise be prepared to undergo an endless series of new beginnings. In her dream, "the wearying infinitives of the wilderness come to an end." Stone walls and rail fences set bounds to the land, and people live, not isolatedly, but close to neighbors, with whom they can share skills and friendship. One swift paragraph capsules in metaphor the entire vision of mankind, the Boone kind and the Diony kind, carving a civilization out of disorder:

The Outlying Spaces

Bees, then, in hives set in neat rows near a dwelling. They gather sweet from the wild growth in the uncleared places and from the pollen of the corn, from the white clover. It would be a civil picture, the hives cut out of well-sawed logs and left to their own devices until the honey made a rich, sweet fatness within. Then a man, Berk Jarvis perhaps, goes among the hives and robs the bees of their harvest, and a woman, herself, Diony, stores the honey in earthen jars of which there would be a plenty.

And then, significantly, since for Miss Roberts "the sovereign part of man is his mind," and Diony is "a creature of mind," the last crowning image of the dream is as follows:

Books stand in a row on a shelf where a narrow beam of light falls through a high casement over a desk where one might rest a volume, where one might sit for an hour and search the terrible pages, looking for beauty, looking for some final true way of life. In them, the books, Man walks slowly down through the centuries, walking on the stairs of the years.

Both the birth and the progress motifs are reiterated with the birth of Tom Jarvis to Diony, which records at once an ending to the old way and the beginning of a new phase of Diony's growth. In parallel with the birth of Tom, the symbolic overtones of the following passage focus on Diony's intense participation in nature, and delicately suggest the interpenetration of man and nature:

The birds had come back from wherever they had been and their morning twitter and clatter, their shrill cries and whistled notes, their pure flute-calls, were blended and severed to flow apart and mingle together through all the early hours of the day. The crab-apple trees against the hill beyond the creek tossed about in the wind and flung out pink and white flowers that spread white in the sun, or, blown all together away from the wind, they turned over and about and were obscured to burst again into wide

61

blooming when the wind eased and gave them a brief calm. The hawthorns, the wild haw trees, had put white flowers out beyond their brittle thorns and they made a sweet scent that blew with the wind that came up from the west by the way that the creek ran. New spring winds swept over the fort and over the forest, any they beat Diony's skirt in a quick rhythm when she went without and tossed the ends of her shawl where they were frayed, bathing all her flesh with a quick desire for more life and a delight in all that she had.

Oh, it was a new day in a new world.

This passage marks Diony's leap into a new self-realization and a reaffirmation of life—both hers and the new life she has borne. Nature, itself, seems to be at one with itself, and it too gives the impression of being on the brink of new creative adventures.

But when Diony has come to believe the persistent reports of Berk's death in the wilderness, in a climactic scene she wanders outside the stockade and spends the night with the wind of the wilderness laying its alien touch upon her: "The land reached away beyond her knowledge and beyond her power to imagine it. The infinitives of life, beetles and owls and animals, leaves and throbbing trees, endlessly growing, oppressed her, and she was afraid, less of the wolf-cries toward the south than of the indefinite earth." And as the night draws on, her awareness of her position in the universe becomes crystallized to a small lucid point:

She sat for some time on a log, the owls crying continually and the furtive steps of beasts crackling the twigs about her. She continually remembered on her side that the whole mighty frame of the world had no being without a mind to know it, but over this lay another way of knowing, and she saw clearly how little she could comprehend of those powers on the other side, beyond the growth of the herbs and the trees, and to sense the hostility of the forest life to her life, and to feel herself as a minute point, conscious, in a world that derived its being from some other sort. The indefiniteness of the outside earth, beyond herself, became a terror.

Again, as in the earlier description of spring, nature offers correspondences which may serve as a source of self-knowledge to the creative spirit, and when Diony returns to the stockade in the morning, we are elliptically told: "No one offered comment on her passing and none knew what way she had been or how far she had gone." However, it is clear that this episode is similar to Theodosia Bell's descent into hell; Diony, shaving her life down to "a minute point," on the very edge of surrender to the chaos around her, does not become "lost" but finds within her the blind faith to continue life.

And in the final chapter, when Berk tells of his adventures among the Ojibway, we hear once again the theme of *The Time of Man* and *My Heart and My Flesh*. To the Indians who would have eaten his flesh to gain his strength, Berk's speech says that the strength is from within, but it is not of the flesh.

" 'You put me in your kettle and you'll not eat one bite of my strength. You'll eat ne'er a thing but my weak part and you'll breed weakness in your bones. Iffen you don't learn better ways to make strength,' I says, 'you are all doomed and you'll all go in the kettle of some better kind. . . . When life goes outen me,' I says, 'the strong part goes too, and I take it wherever I go when I go from here. . . . You couldn't eat ne'er a bit of it. Whe'r I go to heaven or whe'r I go to hell or whe'r I go no place at all, whenever I go from here my strength goes along with me. I take my strong part and you'll never get it inside your kettle and you couldn't eat it into your mouth. God,' I says, 'what a dunce race it is here, to think it could eat strength the like of that.' "

Herald to Chaos

The Enoch Arden situation at the end of *The Great Meadow,* when Berk returns to find Diony married to Evan Muir, is, I think, the one weakness in the novel. It is clear from Miss Roberts' journal notes that she planned it to serve as a resolution of her major themes—the founding of Harrodstown, the birth of the American republic, and Diony's realization of her strength and her limitations—limitations which could be supported by the complementary Boone strength of Berk Jarvis. Unfortunately, the distinction between Evan Muir and Berk Jarvis is not dramatically vivid enough for the reader to perceive immediately the significance of Diony's dilemma. In the novel, the difference between Evan Muir and Berk Jarvis is fuzzily realized. They are both strong men, brave and industrious; Berk is perhaps more reckless than Evan Muir. But, in her private notes, Miss Roberts is quite clear in distinction:

> Berk—Hair light brown. He is six feet in height and grows broader as he develops. . . . A crooked ripple in his smile, a hook in it that caught at a woman's breath . . . little learning. The forward darting, hazzardous [sic] spirit.
>
> Berk represents art.
>
> Evan Muir—A large strong industrious man—Healthy and strong. His smile came readily and lingered, but it could never take the winged crookedness Berk's took. Gray eyes, dark hair. Domestic, quiet, easily predicted.

With these notations as a clue, we can readily read back into the novel examples of the differences between the two men: Berk's lonely pride and labor in the building of the house, his impulsive thirst for vengeance, his abrupt direct manner, and even his name;[6] and on the other hand, the quiet, square domesticity and kindly, easygoing manner of

The Outlying Spaces

Evan Muir. With this reconsideration, Miss Roberts' further note makes much more sense: "Berk, the type of strong-thewed leader, swift in thought and wily, revengeful, a warrior, woodsman, hunter, tireless as the wolf. Large, strong, kind but relentless, driving Diony beyond herself, driving Man forward, thrust outward and forward through the trees and the stones." But, if the realization of this distinction depends on Miss Roberts' journal notation—if the reader cannot feel within the novel itself that Diony's choice is a significant one, integral to the meaning of the novel—then the final episode has a note of contrived artificiality which mars the otherwise harmonious development of the themes.

In the last scene, as Diony sits alone in the house on Deer Creek, Miss Roberts ties together the major strands of the novel in Diony's reflections:

For a little while she felt that the end of an age had come to the world, a new order dawning out of the chaos that had beat through the house during the early part of the night. Her thought strove to put all in order before she lay down to sleep. She felt the power of reason over the wild life of the earth. Berk had divided the thinking part of a man from the part the Ojibways would have put into their kettle and into their mouths. . . . Boone said that he was never lost, she reflected. Boone moved securely among the chaotic things of the woods and the rivers. Beyond her picture of Boone, unlost, moving among the trees, she saw Berk standing before the redmen far in the north, crying in their faces, "You will not put me into your pot. . . . Whe'r I go to heaven or whe'r I go to hell or whe'r I go nowhere at all, I take my strong part with me. . . ." The whole mighty frame of the world stood about her then, all the furniture of the earth and the sky, she a minute point, conscious, soothing the hunger of a child. Boone, she contrived, was a messenger to the chaotic part, a herald, an envoy there, to prepare it for civil men.

65

And thus the creation of order out of chaos, the thrusting forward of man into areas unknown that he may impose a form upon them, and the kind of strength which realizes itself in being a "minute part, *conscious*" in an unconscious world, revitalizing itself over and over again in an endless series of beginnings and ends—all these ideas fuse into the picture of Diony suckling her child in a small shelter of civilization on the borders of the wilderness. The same heroic tones of the classical epic that we heard in *The Time of Man* and *My Heart and My Flesh* are heard again in this "historical novel" of the eighteenth-century settlement of Kentucky. The ideals so eloquently set down in the logical propositions of the Declaration of Independence are herein graphically dramatized in an effective modern heroic form.

HE SENT FORTH A RAVEN (1930): The Curse and the Covenant

IN HER SIXTH NOVEL, *He Sent Forth a Raven*, Miss Roberts returned to the epic scale on which her earlier successes were framed. *He Sent Forth a Raven* is her most ambitious novel, written at the height of her creative power, embodying the heroic sweep of *The Great Meadow* and the torturously introspective frankness of *My Heart and My Flesh*. It is unique in Miss Roberts' work, in that it combines both ways of viewing the universe; it reflects life from the seeing point of the inmost soul of a man, and it rises to the outer edges of the cosmos to peer down at the vast harmony of past, present, and future, of which the long struggle of mankind to progress is but one small aspect. Its symbolic referents suggest the grandest themes in the heritage of western thought—the Prometheus legend of Greek myth, the Biblical flood and the covenant, the blazing prophecy of the Redeemer, and "the hideous and intolerable allegory" of *Moby-Dick*. It projects into the reader's experience the widest range of fully fleshed characters which Miss Roberts was ever to achieve in a novel, without sacrificing the immediacy of character revelation inherent in her mode of subjective narrative focus. It stands as Elizabeth Madox Roberts' noblest attempt to realize the high aspirations for which she labored as an artist: "to increase one's hold on all the out-lying spaces which are little realized in the come and go of every day."

To find a vehicle of sufficient flexibility for this novel, Miss Roberts was forced to revise her characteristic techniques. She retained the device of the episodic development of her heroine, used so successfully in *The Time of Man* and *The Great Meadow,* to it she added the tone of fierce anger which we saw used so effectively in the inward vision of *My Heart and My Flesh.* Then, instead of developing her heroine on a wandering odyssey, she placed Jocelle Drake in a small, isolated community which could be treated as a microcosm, a kind of landlocked *Pequod.* And in the first sentence of the novel—the statement of Stoner Drake's first vow—she establishes a fairytale atmosphere within which her poetic symbols are all but freed of prosaic restraints, and she is able to create characters larger than life who can walk with ease on the level of universal meanings.

Since the novel attempts to do more than any other work of Miss Roberts, and since it has been the source of much confusion in critical interpretation,[1] I shall try to make clear

the three main lines of action in the novel, how they inter-
relate, and how they fuse. When this is completed, I think
we shall be able to recognize in this novel the culminating
achievement of Miss Roberts' developing thought and artistry,
and the justness of the perception by the late Professor Grant
Knight: "*He Sent Forth a Raven* reveals more of Elizabeth
Roberts than does any other of her novels, more of her
exquisite sense of reality, her bewilderment with things as
they are, her lyric anger, her slight vein of madness, her faith
in man's redemption."[2]

The Prologue begins with the dramatic statement of
Stoner Drake's vow: "Stoner Drake made a vow, solemnly
spoken, weighted with passionate words. If Joan Drake should
die he would never set his foot on God's earth again." The
major theme of the novel—man in passionate defiance against
the immutable laws of nature—thus explodes in the very first
sentence. Stoner Drake defies God to exercise his fickle power
over life and death, and when Joan dies, he reiterates this vow:

"I know every field and know how far each goes, up and down,
and what limestone is on the under side. God knows I know. But
so help me God, I'll never set foot on earth again. No man will
persuade me. I'll stay here and if God so desires he can rot me of
my whole flesh. He can put thistles in my mouth for food and
he can sink my acres into the bottomless pits of weeds and hell."

The remainder of Chapter I is a kind of introductory dramatis
personae, moving backward and forward in time, and presented through the selective vision of the heroine, Jocelle.
This chapter is much more effectively welded to the body of
the novel than is the Prologue in *My Heart and My Flesh*.
The perceiving mind is the protagonist's and the material
touched upon is germane to the action of the novel. The

description of the fourteen-room country mansion in which Stoner Drake has voluntarily isolated himself, the reminiscent glimpse of Joan Drake with her passionate vitality, the introduction of Martha the Curfew, and the entry of the young Jocelle into the life at Wolflick thrust the reader into the environment in which the action will unfold, and establish the symbolic connotations of the place and the characters. The isolated old house with its nautical bridge is like a ship in a desolate ocean:

The land rolled in broad undulations of green if the season were moist, or of brown during the dry autumn months, and the landscape was not unlike the swell of an active sea, lifting in large billows or sinking into a trough. . . . Wolflick became year by year a more remote place, lying far, on a crossroad, scarcely visited except by those who had some urgent need to go there.

And to this is added the lonely figure of Stoner Drake:

Drake walked up and down this staircase, the master of the house. His strong step was often heard beating the treads of the stairs. Above, he walked the length of the upper hall to a small door at the rear that gave onto a small balcony looking toward the barnlots and the fields. He wore slung about his shoulder a strap supporting a short hunting horn.

This figure, "housed within walls, blowing wild notes on a conch-horn," bears an unmistakable resemblance to Melville's Ahab. The final section of Chapter I introduces the eight-year-old Jocelle, with her childish but sensitive imagination. She describes to her grandfather "The Place," which she has invented out of her geography book, and he repictures it for her:

"The water sparkles in the sunlight. Spreads like a sheet of silver over stone. A white tower, she says. A long marble stair

69

goes up to the top where you can look out. You'd see the whole of the Place. Gates of smooth wrought-iron. Fine houses along the way, some little and some great, marble fretwork and pillars. Colonnades. Porticoes. Down the river is a door where ships come to land. Stairs go down to the water, broad steps out of granite, any color you say. The sails are made of blue or red or yellow."

But when Jocelle, carried away by the miraculous vision which they have created together, tries to solidify that vision, saying: "God is there," Stoner Drake destroys "The Place" out of his bitter disillusionment:

"Away with you. There's no such. There's no such city. Go on with your lies. Go on. Pattern got by men. Out of his befuddled life. What's he? On one side he's a pulen, unknowen brat. On the other he's a senile, slobberen, totteren, forgotten old man. Who wants to be such a crawlen thing? A new-born, unborn, who wants to be, a unknowen foetus, a snake, a lizard, a blob of greasy slime, proto, proto, proto? What's a city but a hog-wallow of noise and sellen filth? . . . Go on away. Out of my sight."

The major characters are thus established at Wolflick in their characteristic positions: Martha, raking the coals of the fire, as in "some useless and imperative ceremony"; Stoner Drake, bitterly powerful in his cynical withdrawal into himself; and Jocelle, bewilderedly attempting to piece together some order out of the strange house in which she has come to live.

Chapter II moves in time back to 1903 when Jocelle is seven years old, and the remainder of the novel is a chronological account of life at Wolflick until the birth of Jocelle's daughter in 1920. The first level of action has a twofold direction, the first being the odyssey of Jocelle, and the second, the epic story of Stoner Drake's challenge to the gods, with

The Outlying Spaces

Jocelle serving as his Ishmael. Jocelle's story, on this level, is similar to the stories of Ellen Chesser and Diony Hall. Jocelle continually thrusts her growing personality into the crucible of experience, accepting all the vagaries of life, the good and the evil, the true and the false—growing along the principles of harmonious development in a manner we have become accustomed to in Miss Roberts' work. From her earliest recollections in Anneville to her final self-realization in the last pages of the novel, Jocelle moves lightly within the chaos of conflicting passions and dread finalities of chance and circumstance, imposing the order of her being in a positive affirmation of the life force. Her life is a moving document of Miss Roberts' "life is from within" principle, and she takes her high place as one of Miss Roberts' steady, integrative creators of order.

The ordeal of Jocelle's early childhood is suggested in a few swiftly drawn scenes, such as the following poignant portrayal of the terrors of growth:

One day Jocelle's mother looked at her growing frame and said that her dress had become too small. The gaze that accompanied this searching speech entered the scanty garment and measured there the slowly lengthening limbs and the broadening form of the seven-year-old child. Then Jocelle hated her increased frame and she would look down with shame upon her hands and legs that seemed coarse and large. She would try to draw her thin knees under her dress when she sat down. . . . A conviction had been settled upon her; she must not outgrow her clothes. Her life in the town seemed temporary then, a season of unwanted growth, and this illusion of impermanence was strengthened by the knowledge that her mother did not own the house in which she lived. Her mother owed rent for the house. The knowledge of rent which was now and then unpaid for several paying days, weighing heavily upon her, forbade her to grow, but suddenly, from time to time, she would know that more growth had come to her.

But after her mother thrusts her, unannounced and uninvited, into Wolflick, she grows into the pattern of its life, awed but unafraid. The account of Jocelle's childhood and early adolescence is one of Miss Roberts' attempts to present with the immediacy of the actual perception the growth of a living personality; this growth is shaped from without, as in the influence of Jocelle's environment on her concept of what truth is, but it also shapes from within, as in the sudden uninfluenced vision of truth itself. As a little girl she is fond of telling lies in order to protect herself from punishment or to increase her sense of importance; but suddenly, in an irrational, intuitive way, truth, and a desire for truth, become basic to her:

> It came first as if it were a mental apparition, undefined, but with it came a wish or a will or a desire. She wanted to have this which she imperfectly sensed or conceived; she determined that she would have it. Candor appeared to her, as divided from secrecy. Later, after the passion for truth came, she grew into some partial knowledge of what truth might be, gathering this from what lay around her.

Again, as in the description of Jocelle's early childhood at Anneville, Miss Roberts sketches the late adolescence and education of Jocelle at the Seminary with swift, economical images. She is seen in classes, in games with other girls, in her first young love, as an unindividuated unit merged into a larger group, happy in the security of group anonymity. The cycle of growth here is quite similar to that which we observed in both Ellen Chesser and Theodosia Bell. Miss Roberts evidently believed that after the instinctive assertion of identity in childhood (compare Ellen Chesser's "Here I am," or Jocelle's lying), the adolescent needs to immerse himself into the life of the group, absorbing from the resultant sense

72

of "belongingness" the strength and confidence to emerge from the group as a realized personality. Here at the Seminary we find Jocelle "one of the bright wool caps" on the campus:

Through her sense of the experimental music that was forgotten, its discords, falling sweetly unblended through the halls, of gentle professors who admonished kindly and praised her well for work sufficiently done, she saw herself as reflected and reflecting endlessly, her life pitched now to the gentle fervor of the girls, her mates. Herself in her glass where her bright brown hair shone, brushed each evening until it glistened, bound by day with a bright ribbon fillet and put on her head in braid or up-pinned curls, she would carry the image. The girls wore peach-basket hats in the spring.

And in the scene of the graduation dance there is a gentle irony and a penetrating perception in the description of Jocelle leaving her group and going forth into a new life:

Jocelle marched with Patterson, and their lanterns made a pink glow on their faces. . . . They led the long trail of faint fire over the close-cropped grass, making the pattern for the rest, walking before, doubling the design in a long thread that trembled, that fluted in and out through the soft June dark. They talked of where they would be the next year, not knowing, being vaguely afraid of the unknown.
"Anyway, I'll still be Jocelle."
"And I'll be Miles."
Walking thus, and in delight, they went before in the midnight procession, going with their dim paper lanterns into the dark lawn.

There is something very similar to Diony's "rebirth" in Jocelle's delicate emergence from her schoolmates.

The crisis in Jocelle's development, which corresponds to Ellen's desertion by her lover and to Diony's night in the

73

wilderness, comes when she is raped by her cousin. Like Ellen, she is first stunned with anguish and then gripped by violent anger. When her grandfather asks her what war means, she replies:

"Violence. . . . Men mad at life because they're about to leave it. A man you hate drags you to a flat ledge and piles stones on you. Chokes your cry back in your throat. Struggle until your breath gives out. 'I'm on my way to battle,' he says. Your fingernails torn out by the roots. That's what it means. My tongue pulled out of my throat and thrown out to the hound dogs behind the kitchen. A man with tusks that stick out of his jaw. On his way to battle, stopped to say good-by. . . . wiped off his filth on me. That's what war means."

But Jocelle overcomes and successfully absorbs her violation, withdrawing into herself to find the same source of power which enabled Miss Roberts' earlier heroines to survive:

Lying in the semi-dark of the shuttered room. . . . Jocelle would be thinking in feverish jargon of the summer, the world outside the farm where war was being prepared. Encampments, enlistments, embarkments, military jargon, war readiness, propaganda to enlist citizen action. In the barnyard behind the stable a hen was cackling, having laid an egg, screaming over the monstrous awfulness of the thing she had done; she had continued life. Through these ready reports and present confusions went a constant theme that ran on a continuous thread—herself, her life, from the first remembered mists of knowing to the present. It swung outward in a curve and arrived at the present moment, making a sharp thrust, and including all of time as known to her.

Jocelle's immersion in nature, particularly as represented by her broods of white Plymouth Rocks, completes her inner rehabilitation, as the rural life of Spring Valley healed Theodosia. The scar seared on her spirit by Walter does not,

74

of course, disappear, but her hatred of him is replaced by a compassion for the "frantic, careless, frightened, fouled, war-shocked man" who could be atomized into such moral chaos. When news is received that he has been killed in France, she can honestly remind herself that "she had not devised death for him."

When Jocelle and Treer are married, they both realize that the war—the larger universal war of hatred, greed, and jealousy—is not over, but in their love for one another, they make a small advance toward peace: "The war is it over? When will it be over?" "We won't care, war or not, outside or in, if we love together." This is a new birth, a further expansion in Jocelle's development; she has absorbed the senseless violence of Walter's act, and emerged stronger and richer out of her pain: "having become a part now of the strangeness that had come to the farm, evil and good being mingled and opposed, being continually in opposition even while they were intertwined and entangled." And with her marriage to John Logan Treer, she goes forward to create a new life on the foundation of her old one. Jocelle and Treer return to live at Wolflick, and with the birth of her child, Jocelle evaluates her life:

In the drowsy hours that followed Jocelle pondered the child, and the life she had thus far lived, the end and the beginning, the flight of Catharine, the long outward flowing arc of Martha's calamities, and Logan—unremitting, uncaptured, and unhoused. She had drawn life out of Wolflick where a lonely tomb closed over, had closed over Drake years ago. She had been somehow essential to his life and his days.

Like Ellen Chesser, Jocelle extracts her values out of the experience which life offers her, and courageously creates the life which she lives.

The second direction of the novel, certainly coequal in emphasis to Jocelle's plot, is Stoner Drake's story. What was probably Miss Roberts' earliest notation on *He Sent Forth a Raven* is as follows: "Jarvis [Drake] is continually Man unrepenting, uncompromising . . . unwilling, hostile to his narrow fate. Outside are the people of the farms, in debt, patient, taxed beyond their power to pay. They are a great brown legion, unassembled, in unison in suffering but out of harmony. Unable to speak together." At this time Miss Roberts evidently thought of the novel in terms of Stoner Drake's defiance of fate, a defiance which she meant to stand for the proud spirit of man in rebellion against the inhuman forces which limit him. Her initial concept seems to have been socially oriented, since the notation suggests that Drake was to be the articulate representative of all the inarticulate, socially oppressed masses of mankind. However, as the novel began to take form within her mind, the Promethean, or Ahabian, symbol becomes mixed with reverberations of *King Lear*, and the setting becomes less realistic and more poetic; thus, a later structural plan for the novel:

1. Progress in his vow. . . . At first a passionate rebellion against Deity for the loss of a woman. . . .
2. A fierce rebellion but less personal. . . . Uncompromising pity for Man in his losses and his defeat, his aging body and enfebled [*sic*] mind. A total defiance of God and all the gods.
3. Pity for man that he would make such a vow. Infinite pity for all men, for all mental weakness.

However, by the time Stoner Drake makes his second vow after learning of Jocelle's rape, the contending archetypal elements in his characterization have become so intermixed, as we shall see, that the novel took a quite different turn in the writing. The third step in Miss Roberts' note is achieved

76

not through Stoner Drake's self-realization, but by the pitiable spectacle he himself furnishes—a burnt-out old man, permanently bent in the defiant posture of revolt, unable to recall why or for whom he made such a vow.

On this first level, then, we have a realistic novel, written in the middle of the depression, chronicling the life of a farm family from the turn of the century to the middle of the 1920's. What has been called "the agony of our time" is always in the background; the first World War, the "boom," the "bust," the ordeal of America's forcible change from an agrarian individualistically oriented nation to a world power in an intensively capitalistic, industrial world. The ideological struggle arising from this change forms one of the subthemes of the novel, which rejects both the "rugged individualism" of Stoner Drake and the "mob-man" ideology voiced by John Thomas. In terms of the novel, John Thomas' concept is obviously abhorrent, since it is based on a denial of the spiritual potential within every man. It substitutes authority and restraint for the free creation of individual life patterns. Stoner Drake's individualism, although incomparably more noble than this, is found to be impractical for the changing world, which is inexorable in its demands. Drake has no control over the wars, military and economic, which rage across the world's surface. There is no place where he can escape the violence from the outside world, and although he encloses himself in the remote security of Wolflick, the war follows him there, searing the inmates of his house with its hot breath and wresting his property out of his hands. In John Logan Treer's theory of "fellowmenship," the doctrine of "the co-operative man," Miss Roberts offers her solution to this major problem of our times.[3] The cooperative man, for Miss Roberts, will be able to be himself, different or like,

strange or familiar, but his sense of communal responsibility
will enable him to survive and build a society of free indi-
viduals. Treer's is the prophecy of the new man:

> "It's my belief we'll have a new man. Before another decade
> He'll begin. . . . The upstanding, intelligent man. No bathos.
> No tears. We won't know where he was born. We'll know him
> for what he thinks. No man of sorrows. A man of sound sense.
> He'll stand up in his world. Old sculpture *pathétique* can go!
> Loose-jointed *ecce homo!* One protoplasm is like another proto-
> plasm, and why all the stir about the birth? Life is what we want.
> Where's the life of the man? we'll ask. . . . We'll have a new man.
> Good sense and a just peace. No blubber. Able to pool his
> interests with his neighbor's. The co-operative man."

The second line of action in the novel, the Biblical or
cosmic line, parallels the first. Professor Knight suggests a
skeletal synopsis: "out of the flood (World War I), Noah
(Stoner Drake) sent forth a raven (Jocelle) to go to and
fro over the void (post-war society). Later . . . will come . . .
'somewhere or somehow' the Redeemer."[4] This is in essence,
I think, the allegorical meaning of the novel on this second
level, but Professor Knight's comment can be both amplified
and qualified. Stoner Drake is quite definitely, in part, a
Noah figure, but where Noah was favored by God in being
allowed to save himself and his family by taking sanctuary in
the Ark, Stoner Drake defies God and voluntarily imprisons
himself in his ark. Noah acts in humility, acquiescing to
God's inexplicable will because God is "wholly other," and
man's faith is to obey; Stoner Drake is a Noah in rebellion—a
Noah with vengeance in his heart against Him who sent the
Flood. Indeed, Stoner Drake, like Ahab before him, is
goaded past sanity by the fatal horn of the either/or dilemma;
God must exist in humanly comprehensible terms (that is,

78

Drake's terms) or he cannot be allowed to exist at all. Thus his monomania fluctuates between the poles of absolute nihilism and self-aggrandizing humanism. The figure of Drake, as mentioned before, seems to have absorbed such furious contrarieties in the writing that a strict allegorical reading is not possible.

The "raven" which is sent forth from the ark to make a first settlement in the wilderness beyond the ark is Jocelle. Like Boone in *The Great Meadow*, she is a herald to chaos, a hardy trailblazer who goes before, so that the dove may follow bringing peace. And the void over which she flies to and fro is not just "post-World War I society," but the total disorder of modern life. Jocelle is early identified with the raven of the title:

She was unnoticed, about nine or ten years old, at a small table near the hall door. She would lift in mind through the air to hover at each man's shoulder when he spoke, a bird of strong wings and sharp beak, black and invisible, going to and fro above their heads, over their breasts, including them and herself to itself, in their voices, moving with their words, never at rest, a flutter of ruffled feathers with their querulous words, a croaking cry with their protests, a pulsing of quiet wings when they brooded long over some opinion.

Jocelle, then, is not only to go forth at the end—into postwar society—she is from the first the observer and coordinator of life at Wolflick.

And Wolflick, the ark, is a microcosm where faith and atheism contend for the soul of Stoner Drake. Out of the fields comes Jack Briggs, a journeyman preacher who has been ordered in a revelation to go forth to the countryside, preaching Genesis viii.22 to all the people. He is a simple, barefooted man with the odor of sheep about him, and his

79

attachment to Wolflick is an antithetical balance to Dickon, the mechanistic rationalist:

"While the earth remaineth, seedtime and harvest, and cold and heat, and summer and winter, and day and night shall not cease. . . . And the fear of you and the dread of you shall be upon every beast of the earth, and upon every fowl of the air, upon all that moveth upon the earth, and upon all the fishes of the sea; into your hand are they delivered. Every moving thing that liveth shall be meat for you; even as the green herb have I given you all things."

Briggs has heard of Stoner Drake's vow and he determines to "preach him back outen hell if he's so headed." Significantly enough, Stoner Drake allows the preacher to remain at Wolflick. Dickon's book, *The Cosmograph*, is a "confusion of myth and natural phenomena brought together in some scarcely evident coherence, and made to point to a thesis." The thesis, in direct contrast to the divinely ordained unity of Genesis, is an infinite heterogeneity and heteromorphism, "the everlasting otherness of kind building on kind." In violent opposition to the description of the miraculous gift of the universe bestowed upon man in Genesis, Dickon summarizes *The Cosmograph* as follows:

Thus we see that Man, the upstart, the prig of the universe, holds no place. Not even a cog among the wheels. The whole mechanism turns, grinding out forms to pitch them over as the engine goes humming along at a merry pace, and nothing in the whole panoply of phantasmagoria cares if he falls out or in, but you might hear a thundering guffaw on Mount Olympus when he tumbles headlong back into Chaos.

Thus Stoner Drake, emblem of man in rebellion against the inscrutability of the workings of nature, is flanked by oppos-

80

The Outlying Spaces

ing extremists. One exhorts him to lay down his pride and accept the universe because it is good; the other argues that he should forget his pride and accept the universe because he is unimportant and his defiance is that of a spoiled child.

John Logan Treer, the county farm agent, enters Wolflick as a healer, and Jocelle pictures him in her mind as a centaur:

He was riding, unshod, on swift horse limbs, little feet, thin shanks, strong thighs, his hair thrown up in a wind. He was standing, feet drawn together, Chiron, the good centaur, chanting a line . . .:

> "Give me a spark of Nature's fire,
> That's all the learning I desire."

Chiron, renowned for his skill in medicine, is Jocelle's image of Treer, plausibly enough suggested by her first view of him, ministering to the sick animal. But Treer has as well a theoretical potion for the sickness of mankind, a possible cure for the virulent diseases of hatred, violence, and jealousy which have plagued the human race since its inception. In terms of Professor Knight's Biblical analogy, the dove which is to follow, "somewhere or somehow," the Redeemer, is symbolized in John Logan Treer, of whom Jocelle says: "Came to me out of the foot-rot of the sheep. . . . Out of the sour old ewe sick on the stable floor." Treer, the healer, the prophet of "fellowmenship," bears an obvious similarity to that other leader of a spiritual revolution based on love, Christ:

He [Treer] sat beside her, and he began to tell her of what had happened in the months past, saying there was not time now to tell. He made a hurried report of passages from one place to another, of injustice, of harried surmises, of personal ambitions and political blunderings and the kindness of friends. He had not wanted her to know of the humiliations and degradations

81

put upon him. He had been hissed in a public square. He might
not be able to find a place to work, employment, for a long time,
for he had been despised as a slacker, as one outside the vast
group and classed with the enemy. He was outside, he supposed,
but, he cried out suddenly: "I ought not to have been. They'll see
it after awhile. I was inside. I was at the very heart of the age,
at the beginning of what's to come after."

On this level, the visionary level, we find a passionate faith
in the redemption of man, a renewal of the covenant which
insures the eternality of seedtimes and harvesttimes, pointing
toward the ever-beckoning ideal of "peace on earth, good will
toward men."

Jocelle, in the meantime, moves softly among all the
antagonists, absorbing from all and contending with none.
In her bureau she keeps both Dickon's *Cosmograph* and the
closely written manuscripts which expound John Logan
Treer's theories. Jack Briggs shaves his beard for her, since
he has heard it said that "hair is not pleasant to a young girl."
Stoner Drake adds to her repository of gifts and confidence
by bestowing upon her an old family relic, an iron lantern,
first fashioned and used in the original settlement of Fort
Harrod by "common men," as Drake says, "who did an
uncommon thing." Working side by side with Martha, or
hurrying swiftly to answer Stoner Drake's call on the conch
horn, Jocelle nurtures the growing love for Treer within her,
and quietly keeps order in this divided house.

The conflict between Briggs and Dickon reaches its climax
in the scene following Jocelle's wedding, when the argument
turns into a physical struggle and Drake finally enters the
battle to eject Dickon. But, though Briggs attempts to press
his advantage by preaching salvation and projecting a picture
of Wolflick in flames, Drake turns away. The field is left,

then, to Jocelle and Treer, in whose marriage the life-creating principles of courage as the condition of individual existence and love as the salvation of society are united.

Preacher Briggs' prophesy of the burning of Wolflick is the final link in a chain of symbolic references to fire which runs through the entire novel, and may be in part a remnant of an earlier version in which Miss Roberts actually included the burning of Wolflick. The importance of the theme is pointed to by the presence of the "Curfew" passage in the prologue. Its most explicit development is in the scene when the entire family, with Dickon and Briggs, is sitting around the dining table, and J.T. asks Stoner Drake the climactic question: "What would you do if the house should catch fire? House burn down?" The question reverberates onto the cosmic plane, as Drake interprets it to be "What will I [man] do when the whole world is drowned in a lake of fire?" This restates the conflict between Dickon and Briggs over Stoner Drake, with Drake caught in an untenable middle position, acknowledging supernal purpose in his defiance of God, and unable to submit to that purpose because he judges it inhuman and unjust. J.T.'s question leads to Stoner Drake's examination of the meanings of fire and the reiteration of his outcry: "There's a mort of unnecessary pain. . . . If God would but talk plain to mankind, say fact, quit mystery." In Drake's inquiry into "fire," he who is given the Promethean nickname "Firebrand" moves from the fire on the hearth to Empyrean fire, and from there to the fierce fire raging on the earth in the form of war and famine:

Empyrean. The light of the upper world, the fire of heaven, the blinding light of the sky. . . . Eyes then. Eyes are the receptacle of light, the mirror of fire, the opposite, the complement, the toward-what. Two little suns in the head of a man made to take in the light of the sun and to turn it into sense. . . .

"These things saith he which hath the sharp sword with two edges: I know . . . where thou dwellest, even where Satan's seat is. . . . He that hath an ear, let him hear what the Spirit saith. . . . The first angel sounded, and there followed hail and fire mingled with blood." The first woe is past: I've read it through time and time again. How can a man untangle this mystery?

Fire, the ultimate destroyer and energizer of life, has a wealth of connotations, ranging from the warm hearthglow to the blinding explosion of gases in the solar system, which make it a fitting symbol for the manifestation of spirit in the material universe. One of its emanations is "light" or "enlightenment," but no man can look steadily into the sun. Drake's investigations lead to no conclusion save bafflement, but the existence of a fierce fire at Wolflick is pointed to in the concluding paragraph of the same chapter:

> Later in the night Martha came back to the fireplace and carefully covered the flames with dead ashes. All were now gone to rest. Above in her room Jocelle heard the scraping of the shovel when the fire in the parlor was covered. The kitchen fire was tended likewise.
>
> Night after night Martha performed this last midnight task. Each fire was visited and each was carefully guarded with dead ashes, each carefully scraped together and covered. The young men called her Curfew then.

Martha the Curfew ("fire coverer") banks the fires each night, lest they rage in total destruction, but she banks them carefully, lest they be entirely extinguished by the surrounding flood.

The third line of action in *He Sent Forth a Raven* can be viewed almost as a sketch of the anatomy of the spiritual personality. The inhabitants of Wolflick can be interpreted not only as a microcosmic abstraction of the world, but as a macrocosm of the individual spirit. The isolation of Wolflick, intensified by Stoner Drake's adamant refusal to "set a foot on God's green earth," suggests the absolute isolation of the individual.

Stoner Drake, "the lonely Will, the wish, the desire of the heart, housed within walls, blowing wild notes on a conch-horn," stands quite naturally, even in the rocklike solidity of his name, for that "proud ghost," the will within the total "I." He is the master of the soul, the giver of orders, the imposer of individuated personality. It is he who brings pride within the spirit, since he cannot bear contradiction or defeat. He is also the energizing flame, the volitive force which insists on life. His characteristic gesture is phallic and commanding: "His fingers were ready to crumple into a fist leaving the index finger free to point, so that, since this gesture came frequently to his hands, Jocelle thought of it as being the man himself, as if his whole body and being focused to a sharp pointing finger."

And he is flanked by Jack Briggs and Sol Dickon, both combatants for his attention. Briggs, with the smell of the beasts upon him, seems to represent simple faith. He is of the earth, without sophistication or logic; but he believes, and his belief is supported with the strength of his entire frame. He has been commissioned to preach Genesis viii.22, and this he does, scarcely understanding the words he has memorized; his influence is based on the brute power with which he believes. Dickon, the "Beelzebub" of *The Cosmograph*, is Briggs' opposite number, reason. He is the carpenter, the advocate of scientific cause and effect. In Jocelle's early glimpse of his room in Anneville, she perceives his elemental

85

nature: "Plain unbelief settled about the remembered spareness of the room, about the clear lamp and the few sheets of unwritten paper. Dickon walked heavily through the emptiness he had devised." He has sought for the cause behind the effect, and the cause behind that cause, until logic has "proved" to him that there is no final cause, no ultimate purpose to anything. Significantly, after the ejection of Dickon, Stoner Drake still does not succumb to Briggs' exhortations. The inference is plain that the will must work with both faith and reason; neither is capable of supplying the other's function. They must be harmonized into effective action.

The figure of Martha is more difficult to interpret on this level, perhaps because it is not completely realized. Her salient characteristic seems to be suggested by her name, that of the sister of Lazarus who was "cumbered about much serving" in contrast to Mary, who heard Jesus' word directly. Martha the Curfew is the housekeeper of Wolflick, the guardian of the fire who tends the fire, but possesses it only by reflection. Although she is cynical and withdrawn,[5] she serves conscientiously, calling down from her room warnings to Jocelle, and it is she who reminds Briggs that he must preach love as well as obedience. In her bitter self-sacrifice, the steady impress of her strength should not be underestimated; although she is unable to restrain the will in any direct conflict, she does check its smouldering fires regularly, keeping the house safe from complete conflagration. In the following description, there seems to me a strong suggestion of the quality of devoted service, or duty:

The shadows gave the mouth by the hearth a broad lateral line that was now fixed and still. The woman at the hearth was carved out of some illumined stone and she looked with steady searching gaze. . . . The statue beside the hearth, carved now in fire, did not yield its gaze, nor did the latitude of the carved mouth shrink or the lines quiver.

John Logan Treer is the last to come within Wolflick, and at that, he is reluctantly given admittance.[6] "He was elusive . . . a scheme, a plan, an ideal." It is difficult to assign him a name, but perhaps the one suggested by Miss Roberts, "ideal," will be as suitable as any other. He is a latecomer and the least understandable to the other faculties of the soul. He is not the kind of ideal projected by the will for its own aggrandizement; he is more that communal ideal —the "fellowmenship" which Miss Roberts felt to be common to all men—and as such, he comes unbidden and even resented by the soul: "He was visionary, militant, melancholy in his concern for mankind and in his thought of himself as being mankind. He was elusive, not to be analyzed, to be comprehended in a mass rather, or left as the source of wonder and surprise."

And Jocelle, finally, is the imagination, the integrative, creative imagination which coordinates the total activities of all the faculties of the spirit. She moves amidst the will, faith, reason, duty, and the elusive ideal, taking from each (Drake's iron lantern, the shaving of Briggs, *The Cosmograph*, the friendship of Martha, and Treer's theories and love) and producing, in turn, something which incorporates an essence of each one of them, but is at the same time something greater than the sum of all of them—new life, Roxanna:

Sleeping, and waking, she [Jocelle] saw within the act of seeing, as if the brain itself were a prism, a crystal-clear design, a mathematical form, and as such common to all men. . . . And thus, a clear design, the mind, common to all men, it pointed an index, to a communal sharing which was religious, the sharing of the common mental pattern where individual traits merged.

And therefore of fear and faith and praise.

In it somewhere or somehow came the Redeemer.

Under this again, under communal devotions and emotions, the lonely will, the wish, the desire . . . the underlying complexity reducible within itself and of itself to the one simple determinate, lonely among its fellows, aloof, arising now to a super-life, the will to believe, to live, to hate evil, to gather power out of emotion, to divide hate from love where the two are interlocked in one emotion, the will to love God the Creator.

Thus, on this third line of symbolic action, there is an amazing parallel to what we have seen to be Miss Roberts' basic theme—the imposition of order on chaos. Just as the raven is sent forth from the Ark, like Boone blazing a Wilderness Road so that mankind can follow subduing nature and creating form where before there was void, so the intuitive imagination of man's soul integrates the incongruities and conflicts of his inmost spirit, creating a harmony and order within, without which he could not exist.[7]

He Sent Forth a Raven is, I believe, a unique novel in twentieth-century American literature. Its universal cosmic scope and its intimate grappling with the most fundamental problems which face modern man give it a depth and breadth possessed by no other contemporary American novel that I know. Although it presses with penetrating honesty into topical problems, it does this in terms of the aesthetic experience, offering no glib solutions or pat dogmas. Its passionate intensity, its deep-lying optimistic faith in the creative potential of man, and its provocative and profound vision, stamp it with the ineluctable markings of exalted artistic inspiration. I believe that *He Sent Forth a Raven* is one of the finest achievements in modern American letters.

CHAPTER FOUR

Elegant Chambers

JINGLING IN THE WIND (1928): *Amor vincit omnia.*

JINGLING IN THE WIND, we are told, was written concurrently with *The Time of Man* and *My Heart and My Flesh* as a kind of spontaneous release from the strenuous pressure of these first two novels.[1] It is a poetic fantasy employing the technique of satire, Miss Roberts' only published work to illustrate her belief that she had the mental and temperamental equipment to become a satirist. Miss Roberts herself makes only the slightest reference to this novel in her private papers; so perhaps the assumption that this is a *jeu d'esprit*, conceived as a means of relaxation and fun, is not unfounded. She writes: "The one reality in this is Jeremy's soul or mind, that alone can be treated seriously."

Satire is most commonly employed as a tool for social and

moral criticism, and, as we know, in the hands of an accomplished satirist, it can be a very deadly weapon. The satirist generally attacks some established institution, tradition, or socially held set of beliefs. But we have already seen that Miss Roberts was not wholly committed to a belief in the objective reality of the external world. Life was, for her, more or less what one was capable of making it, depending on one's creative capacities. Social institutions, traditions, and beliefs had an existence for Miss Roberts, but not the kind of absolute overpowering existence that they possessed for, say, Sinclair Lewis. For the latter, the stupidity which he found in society was of great importance because it operated to stultify those ideals or life qualities which he felt to be significant. Lewis could therefore get angry enough to compose a sustained criticism of society, but the role of social crusader is one in which it is impossible to imagine Elizabeth Madox Roberts. Further, her subjective mode of narration requires an active introspective mind as hero, and we have seen that the focus of her action is never on the outside happening, but on the inner transformation of the happening. Accordingly, we can expect that Miss Roberts' experiment with satire will be a very different thing from what we regard as traditional satire.

For a structural framework she adopts the form of the picaresque novel, using a rather whimsically entangled love quest to get her rogue-hero "on the road" where he can observe what is going on in the world. But then she suffuses this traditional pattern with a combination of farce, fantasy, and poetry, leaving the reader with a concoction that should be drunk swiftly with one's eyes shut. Allan Nevins attempts to explain this mixture sympathetically, as follows: "It is a gentle clouded form of satire, sometimes rather wistful, and

seldom more than reproachful. It is a mockery that shifts
and changes in color and form from page to page, usually
defying analysis. The poetry dances, disappears, and reap-
pears. To enjoy the book the reader must surrender himself
to its capricious humor; its elfish alternation of tenderness
and laughter, its opal combination of fire and vapor, its sudden ascents from rough homeliness to lyricism."[2] Kenneth
Burke, on the other hand, finds nothing to praise in the
novel, except the works which the novel reminds him of:
"The *Jingling* suggests something of Chaucer, *Candide*, and
Alice in Wonderland, but remains a book of no great moment
despite its distinguished antecedents."[3]

I would think that the danger in analyzing *Jingling in the
Wind* would be to take it too seriously. Accordingly, I shall
examine the novel, not as a unified metaphorical statement
of experience—which it isn't—but as a pastiche, parts of which
are wonderful in themselves, and parts of which are interesting in the light they shed on Miss Roberts' other work.

First, let us look at Jeremy's mind, the one reality which
Miss Roberts felt could "be treated seriously." He is the
rainmaker of Jason County, sensitive, devoted to his art, and
seemingly self-sufficient. Both by choice and temperament he
is relatively isolated from the profit-making world:

He was prone to search into the hows of things, the from-
whiches and the to-whats, and this bent shut him off from many
of the more rapid considerations of business and inoculated him
from the profit-taking world, for, while he searched for the
from-which or the toward-what, for a relation or a modality, the
profit had always been taken by some more ready agent.

He possesses seven deadly sins, seven cardinal virtues, twenty-
two phantoms, and is sometimes beset by two witches, three

nymphs, and five fiends. However, these are not particularly
important, since Miss Roberts regards these as the properties
of all men. More significantly: "Pride was his chief enemy,
and this one gave him many an under-thrust when he did not
suspect his presence." We have already seen the effects of
Theodosia's pride in *My Heart and My Flesh*, and, in truth,
the chronicle of Jeremy's plot is really the same as Theodosia's,
played in a comic, minor key. When Jeremy is singing over
his breakfast, we discover his insufficiency:

Jeremy sang again, interrupting his tribute to the universal
Spring, his song raising a pretty allegro before the doors of his
shut heart, carousal that almost awoke another, the inner sleeper.
His song kicked its shins together at last and lay down to rest
at the curb, a dirty little gamin that consorted with the common
grass of the gutter.

Through his pride in his achievements, he has become an
isolated man; his heart is closed to love. The plot action of
the novel will send him on a romantic love quest to open his
spirit, subdue his pride, and fulfill his being.

When Jeremy's friend Josephus returns from the metropolis to tell Jeremy of his adventures, he reveals the fact that
he has fallen desperately in love with one Tulip McAfee, a
girl who is betrothed to a bespectacled gentleman. As he
speaks, Jeremy is enabled to "see" her as though she were
standing before him:

As she stands she is speaking and as she speaks she winds the
blue and green scarf about her hands, and the blue shadows of
the scarf lend bluer shade to her fine-nerved fingers, that are
as sensitive as if they were—as they are—projections of her fine,
swift mind, and when she comes into his presence, all the birds

of a man's heart will begin to sing and the whole sunrise of his soul will begin to dawn in the east.

It is no surprise then that at the end of Chapter Two, Jeremy has unknowingly decided to visit the metropolis:

One morning as he put aside his hat, his hand stayed at the hat-brim, a thin little waif, saying, "Go to the world. Go to the city." The words were flipped half-formed from starved lips and the apparition dived into the cellar of his unconscious thought and went out of his memory altogether.

While Jeremy and his fellow passengers are waiting for the motorbus to be repaired, and whiling away the time by telling stories to one another, Tulip herself appears "in the heart of a cloud, pursued by four or five wild horses." Her unconventional vehicle, as she later explains, was a very volatile Freudian dream. Jeremy is smitten to the depths with love, but he discovers that Tulip has undergone a change in heart since Josephus last observed her. In the story of her life, which she shortly relates, she makes cynical comments about love:

"I have always observed," mused Tulip . . . "that parents derive far more pleasure from the begetting, conceiving, bearing, and rearing of offspring than the offspring derive from being begotten, conceived, born and reared. And in view of the fact that my own begetting, conceiving, bearing, and upbringing yielded me so little of anything which might be described as pleasure, I have often thought that I would be quite justified or forgiven for deriving any pleasure I could from the begetting, conceiving, the bearing and upbringing of some people on my own part, in spite of the fact that this might cause the people themselves some inconvenience. . . . But that is the view held by most adults and I claim no individuality or unique genius in making the statement."

Herald to Chaos

As "the lady with the child" remarks, Tulip has become "what is sometimes described as a hard woman, a 'hard-boiled' virgin." On further examination, Jeremy discovers that the change in Tulip from the sweet young vision of Josephus' dreams to the "hard-boiled virgin" who stands before him has been the result of disillusion in love. The bespectacled gentleman to whom Tulip was engaged had paid court under false colors. As she says: "I found I had yielded to a non-existent personality. I had been willing to mate for life, even eager to so copulate, with the Amalgamated Irrigation Corporation of North America and Europe."

The plot thus takes on complications, the love theme becoming twisted to involve both Jeremy and Tulip. While Jeremy's inner being, so long locked against love, has become open, Tulip has closed herself off, taking up the profession of rainmaker in order to be self-sufficient. There is further complication in the stubborn pride of Jeremy, which will keep him from engaging in an open aggressive courtship: "I shall perhaps discover ways to make myself necessary to her experience, comely to her sight, brave and honorable in her imagination, always feeling the air for signs of hostility, scorn, weariness, or contempt. . . . I will keep myself always in the rear of my affection, at least until I see how the land lies." However, the plot is resolved in the end in the whimsical fashion we might expect. Jeremy becomes the hero of the Rainmakers' Convention, being chosen as "The Rain Bat" to operate the model rain. He discovers, however, that he is only a tool in the whole operation which has been designed on the upper echelons by Tulip McAfee to counter the Anti-Rain evangelism led by James Ahab Crouch. Jeremy swallows his pride somewhat reluctantly and prepares to woo Tulip in the accepted "open" manner. He persuades himself that he is really organizing a new "Masculine Renaissance" which will usher in a new age: "Woman is to be gracious and beautiful, the giver of gifts, co-equal with man but different in office. The woman is going to know again the glory of submitting. Man is to be the ruler in the house." However, this threat is not as distressful as it might seem, because he realizes that "The first step toward a Masculine Renaissance will be the restoration of flattery and chivalry." Thus, love conquers all—both pride and amorous disillusionment, and we are perhaps not wrong to suspect that the ladies have the best of it.

On the satirical side, Miss Roberts evidently chooses the subject of rainmaking in order to ridicule the contemporary battle between "Religion" and "Science" which was raging around the Scopes "Monkey Trial." This can be clearly seen in the following history of rainmaking which Jeremy soliloquizes over:

The population was divided into two masses, those who opposed rain control as a device of the devil, as blasphemous or pagan, and those, the more open-minded or daring, who looked upon the cult as a benefit to man. Of the last group there were again other subdivisions. There were those who held that every man's house is his castle and who advocated independent rains. . . . Then there were those who favored cooperative rains . . ., and thirdly, there were those who advocated standardization. . . . The anti-faction was massed as one marching unit. The evangelists of many sects preached the downfall of the rain counties. Were they not belittling God himself, interfering with His designs and subtracting from His power? A strong anti-lobby was organized. Captions arose, to become the bases of folk songs, as "Your God needs you, join now," and the like. . . .
Now . . . the anti-faction classed their opponents in one group, with the so-called monkey-men and hated and feared all those together, retorting to all of them with the same wit. "God

made man in his own image and God did not look like a monkey,"
they said, or "Taking the prerogative of God they belittle God-
Almighty." "Stealing from God," they said, "stealing God's
rain."

Her caricature of James Ahab Crouch, "the most powerful
evangelist of the day," who spends his time spitting anathemas
at the monkey men, the rain men, and Zelda Tookington,
the "incomparable dancer of the seven veils," seems to draw
on Billy Sunday for its inspiration and its humor.

In general Miss Roberts' satirical attempts in the novel
are directed at the inconsequentiality of most of what passes
for significant activity in the great wide world; and at man's
proneness to avoid the responsibility of his own struggle for
values. The frenzy of the twenties—Prohibition, jazz, advertising, Hollywood, the fads and farragoes of the times (which,
as at all times, make loud noises but never sound beneath the
surface)—are gently lampooned throughout the novel, most
specifically in the scene of the great parade of trivia which
passes by the indifferent spinning spider of culture:

"I have all here in my hands," she was saying, moving forward in an arc, catching the thread, a pause, a movement forward, a whirr of drawn silk. "I have it all here, the whole of
culture. I draw it all out of myself with my long supple fingers,
I pattern it on the air. I make it as I go, but it is made already
within me, spinning. I knot a thread, thus, with the thrust of
my abdomen, spinning, and I knot another, going ahead, making.
This segment here is a science, and this renaissance, or I go thus,
spinning, and here is a psychology of love. Or a university. We
come now to a dark age, a knot here, my long pliant fingers
turning. I draw it out with my hands. A dark age is followed
by an age of enlightenment, and here is a new religion. Votes for
women, moral prescriptions, Egypt, India, Babylon, I make a
knot, a rise and a decline. Morning, noon, mathematics, a one-

god, Isis, I make a knot, St. George, Diana, St. Brigid, war, a
romantic era, an enlightenment, a new art, a new disease, jewelry,
a new vegetable, sin, savagery again, I make a knot, and I am
back again, a new philosophy, a Pyramid."

But although Miss Roberts registers satirical success here
and there, as in her vision of the neon zodiac in which the
constellations spell out advertising slogans, the humor is, for
the most part, either too heavyhanded or too oblique to bite
with the sharp deflating snap of effective satire. She has a
tendency to hold on to a joke too long, or to overwrite when
understatement would better serve her ends.[4] Her employment of farce and her intrusion of too much burlesque, as in
the long unattached episode of Khadija-Pai, concubine to the
Sultan Arhaj-Moomug-Ke, serve only to confuse and—let us
admit it—bore the reader. Similarly, the long-drawn-out
"gland-story" of Zelda Tookington and the mysterious figure
of Mr. Breed have no real function in the novel. The weakness of *Jingling in the Wind* may ultimately lie in Miss
Roberts' failure to find an appropriate structural frame within
which she could develop her themes. The title and the chain
of stories in Chapter II suggest that she may have planned
to keep the novel loosely within a framework modeled on
The Canterbury Tales, but this would account for only one
of her five chapters. And that one chapter is not particularly
good in itself.

However, there is more to the novel than all this. There
is an unbridled ebullience in this book—a singing immersion
into the beauty and music of nature which the free play of
fantasy allows Miss Roberts to achieve. There is a wise
spinning spider, an Irish snake driven out of Ireland by Saint
Patrick, and an articulate life in all things that grow and
crawl. Here is a long sample passage which comes close to

transferring the steady surge of life from the earth to the printed page:

A hen beyond the wire fence then made a soft pretty singing in two tones, four syllables, a song that named her by her own name, "Pertelote," and put an end to the rain, and indeed it was done. The drops stood now on the leaves like fixed crystals, or one slid down a grass leaf and fell into the earth. Pertelote continued her purring song, her name brought into musical discourse and made to argue for the good of moist earth and the general boon of small beetles and soft lush caterpillars that crawl after a shower. A red ant came then out of the tangled grass and ran over a rotted leaf. A little gray hopper sprang across from some sheltered place, but when Jeremy brushed her twig with his heel, she leaped twenty times her length and landed on a plantain leaf, and then to the green spiked flower of the plantain. When Jeremy moved his heel he saw that he had trampled a white fuzzed caterpillar.
"You touched earth lightly with your down," Jeremy began. . . .
The caterpillar could not reply to this except by way of his yellow juice that oozed over a bruised plantain leaf and by way of his writhing head that still held the ghost of life. Pertelote talked again, of the substance of a man and the yellow substance of a caterpillar, putting all that she had to say in the form of a question.
"Per te lo te?"
When he spoke Jeremy felt ungainly and ill-proportioned, awkward among the things of the earth and the wet. His voice would not key to the singing of a toad behind a stone or to the click of a grasshopper's legs. He stood tall and broad out of the wet.

It seems to me that in passages such as these—and there are many in *Jingling in the Wind*—Miss Roberts justifies her title in giving voice to the voiceless growth of the earth and reasserting in affirmative tones the rich organic connection between the life of man and the life of nature. The poetry of her prose reaches its high point perhaps in such passages as that containing the "Life is from within" sentence, where Madame Eglentyne's emblem, "*Amor vincit omnia*," receives a fresh revitalization. On formal grounds of aesthetic harmony, or in terms of effective satire, *Jingling in the Wind* is probably a failure; but these considerations seem somehow unimportant before the salient achievement of the book; it is capable of delighting a reader. For this we should be thankful, for few serious contemporary writers have deigned to recognize the domain of delight as one of their just provinces.

A BURIED TREASURE (1931): Movements in Counterpoint

IT IS USUALLY IMPOSSIBLE to specify with any accuracy the actual physical occurrence which may trigger the creation of a work of art. And even in those few cases where we can be fairly certain that we know the stimulus, our information is still of dubious value in the assessment of the completed imaginative work. One thing that we can do is to measure approximately the distance that separates the end product— polished, complicated, and set into artistic form—from the stark raw material which was its genesis. There is a kind of value in being able to observe the quality of an artist's mind in the process of work. To a certain extent we are able to do this with Elizabeth Madox Robert's fifth novel, *A Buried Treasure*,[1] since there appears among her collection of private papers the following newspaper clipping:

99

Herald to Chaos

While plowing corn on his farm near town on Thursday, June 1, Mr. Sam Bottom found three Spanish dollars and an American half-dollar. The Spanish coins were dated 1784, 1804, and 1820, and the United States coin bore the date 1811.

Mr. Bottom said, "I realized I had a gold mine in my place but it never dawned on me until finding these coins that I owned a silver mine. I expect to dig up every inch of that field and sift the dirt until I find every piece of coin buried there."

It is interesting to speculate on the impact which this newspaper story might have had on Miss Roberts' imagination. The discovery of buried money in a cornfield does not seem enough in itself to enkindle the fires of creativity. But when we add the fact that the buried money dates back to the earliest Kentucky settlements, the news story becomes more provocative. Here is treasure, sunk into rich meadowland for over one hundred years. The vision of generations of hardy settlers, tilling the soil, planting, and harvesting, comes almost inevitably to mind; and the treasure within the earth begins to make an ironic contrast with the treasure that is the earth. The final paragraph of the clipping caps the provocative potentialities of the story with the note of unconscious irony in Mr. Sam Bottom's statement. Here, in miniature, are the elements which must have appealed to Miss Roberts' sense of humor and sense of story. A naive humorless man dedicates himself to a search for treasure on his property, overlooking all the elements which, for Miss Roberts, are the real treasure lodes in life. This is the main contrast of A *Buried Treasure*. And the long-lying heritage of generations symbolized in the old concealed coins is its minor theme.

Because it is more natural for her to work with a heroine

Elegant Chambers

than with a hero, Mr. Sam Bottom (Andy Blair) is relegated to a subordinate position, and his wife, Philadelphia Blair, becomes the focus of the narrative. The minor theme—that of the heritage of generations—is developed in an independent subplot. Miss Roberts is reported to have told Grant Knight that she meant A Buried Treasure to be "an experiment in the presentation of shifting points of view."[2] In the analysis of The Great Meadow we noted that Miss Roberts apparently was searching for a way to overcome the limitations of her intensely subjective mode of narration; this "experiment in the presentation of shifting points of view" is perhaps a logical next step as she copes with the problems of her craft.

The novel is written in five chapters, Chapters I, III, and V being narrated from Philly Blair's point of view, and Chapter II and IV from Ben Shepherd's. The action, from the discovery of the iron kettle filled with treasure, to the denouement on Midsummer Night, takes only a few weeks; the characteristically long development of Miss Roberts' protagonists is thus sacrificed in order to exploit the effect of a single dramatic episode. This is a radical departure from her customary methods of narration. Her use of symbolism is different also from the large designs which we have observed in The Time of Man, My Heart and My Flesh, and The Great Meadow. In those novels the main symbolic patterns emerged from the struggles of man against and within nature; in A Buried Treasure, however, Miss Roberts resorts to the device of investing a physical object with the full weight of her symbolic connotations. The symbolic movement of the novel will depend ultimately on the meaning that the buried treasure takes on for the two major characters, Philly Blair and Ben Shepherd.

The character of Philly Blair is established in the opening

101

chapter—she is a middle-aged woman possessing an extraordinary capacity for empathy, as well as the sensitivity we have come to associate with Miss Roberts' heroines. Philly, like Theodosia and Diony, is engaged in a search into her life pattern attempting to discover what values she possesses and what she lacks. The theme, however, is treated with a much less serious tone than is Theodosia Bell's search. Philly is a mature woman, and experience has given her a perspective on herself, an ironic sense of self-proportion, which Theodosia completely lacked. And Ben Shepherd's observation of the action is fundamentally colored by his adolescent conviction that romance—love, sexuality, beauty—is the exclusive property of adolescence. This doubly ironic frame succeeds in placing Philly's self-examination in a humorous light; indeed, the discovery of a pot of gold has a grotesquely comic quality in itself, and the general atmosphere of the first chapter creates a pastoral lightness, inappropriate to a chronicle of a descent into the soul. We recall that Miss Roberts is reported to have "thought of the book as a comedy in five acts."[3]

Chapter II reverts in time to the day of the discovery of the iron kettle, and Ben Shepherd becomes the focus of the narrative. The timespan of the first two chapters is the same, and the themes developed in these chapters stand in a contrapuntal relation to one another. The buried treasure has impelled Philly to examine herself for strengths and weaknesses, and this, in turn, has engendered in her a feeling of thwarted maternity. She has turned from the buried treasure toward her young cousin Imogene, seeing herself in the girl —young, fecund, in love; her self-search continues in the search for the daughter she never had. Ben Shepherd, on the other hand, comes to the Pigeon River country, trying to know himself through discovering his fathers; he is young, denied admittance to the world of Giles and Imogene, because he is only on the outermost edge of adolescence. His buried treasure, the Shepherd graveyard, leads him, like Philly Blair, to center upon Imogene, trying to find within her the secret of life. And at the end of Chapter II, the two themes are played side by side, as Philly Blair sits with her feet on the iron pot, and Ben Shepherd stands by the doorway with the stolen metatarsus in his pocket. But in the remaining chapters Philly's story and Ben Shepherd's subplot are not so well integrated. The third chapter, told from Philly's point of view, advances both stories; the fourth takes up where it leaves off and brings Ben's story to a close; the fifth, Philly's again, resolves the complications of the plot and provides a symbolic resolution of the novel's underlying themes.

Philly's story begins with the discovery of the treasure,[4] and her immediate determination to "do something" with this new prosperity to help her young cousin points both to Philly's thwarted maternity and to the theme of sex as a principle of creativity:

Imogene was like herself in many things, and while Philly rubbed the small goldpiece until it was clean, she felt as if she were the same, identical with Imogene, as if the turn of her hand and the pressure of her fingers on the little rag that cleaned the gold of tarnish were Imogene's own. Then a passion arose within her, a clear and swift determination to make a better way of life for Imogene, to make her free to have something for herself, to give her the pleasure of a lover.

Philly has a moment of clear perception in which she understands the motivations which drive Sam Cundy to deny all suitors access to Imogene. Philly looks at Imogene and sees instead Lispy, Imogene's mother—dead these seven years:

Then Philly saw a clear shape, evenly defined and sharply rounded; it was the hold Sam Cundy had on Imogene and the reasons for his hard demand, shaped now to a conclusion in her mind, as clear as if she saw a pictured object. Cundy wanted to keep Imogene in his house. He would never consent to have her marry. He wanted her about, under his eyes, near his hands. She looked like her mother; he held her confused with the other woman in his mind; he would not let her go.

Sam Cundy's love for his daughter has become a perverted love—perverted because it denies life to Imogene in order that Sam Cundy may retain his grasp on the dead. So, in arranging Imogene's marriage, Philly is not only giving happiness to Imogene, whom she identifies both with herself and with the daughter she has never had, but is helping the creative life principle to triumph over a destructive and life-denying principle.

The symbolic functions of the treasure itself are quickly developed. While Philly and Andy keep their discovery a secret, planning to reveal it to the neighbors at a party, Andy removes the pearls, keeping them to himself. Philly wonders "that he should take out some part and retain it from their common keeping," but she reflects that he has had prior claim to the treasure, and besides she is "amused and pleased that he should have a secret." When Andy asks her to find an old key, however, she looks also for "the small sack containing the two pearls":

> She fitted keys into little slits and tried to make them turn bolts over, and she went again to look into the smallest and most secret place of the house, the secret drawer in the dark cubbyhole, remembering then that Susie [her sister] had six children and if she had lost there would be six to help her find. She was weary and warm from the search, having been up and down stairs and ladders, bending and searching and feeling, and

104

she thought here of Andy as having been too stingy to give her any children, as having held back a part of what he should have given her, as taking what he wanted and holding back some final little thing.

The search into secret drawers and the inserting of keys into locks suggests a sexual significance for this passage, which is confirmed by her reflection on the productivity of her sister and her own barrenness. When we remember that Philly is searching for two pearls sewn into a little sack, the general meaning of this passage becomes fairly clear. The theme is developed as her search continues:

The deep gray twilight of the cubbyhole was darkened by her own shadow, for she had crawled into the small doorway. Her fingers fumbled among old spider webs that had become heavy with dust and age. She reached into dust and mold and her fingers took meanings and minute forms from the bits that she fumbled, the ends of herself meeting the fine ends of these withered things and bringing a picture of what they would appear to be if they were seen, so that she smelt the feel of them, crawling into the blackness. Thus her double search, for a key and a sack, became a triple search in which she probed Andy minutely to see where he lacked.

The fumbling in the dust and mold, "the ends of herself meeting the fine ends of these withered things," is a metaphorical self-examination. Finding a lack in herself—the fact that she is barren—she turns her examination on Andy to find out what it is that he lacks. The two pearls are quite obviously a symbol of male fertility, but we must remember that they are just one part of the buried treasure.

Later, she stealthily searches Andy's body at night, finding the pearls strapped to the forepart of his trunk by a piece of tape, and wonders if he carries them thus "to make up somehow for whatever he lacked." Her delight in what Andy has done grows as she thinks about it, and he becomes, in her eyes, an "increased" man. Philly is alarmed when she finds that the pearls are missing, and immediately it becomes clear to her that Andy has given them to Hester Trigg, "for Hester could easily get the best that any man had."

It is only after the disappearance of the pearls arouses Philly's jealousy and pride that the full significance of the treasure held in common by Philly and Andy is made explicit in Philly's clear sudden realization:

She saw it from a long way off, but it had once been near at hand, it had once been her own to have and to know. . . . It was a knowledge of herself as being lovely both without and within, as having inside herself a warm flow of blood and little tremors of delight. Delight was beautiful and she had a fine measure of it inside herself somewhere and everywhere. Andy was near her to make her know how lovely she was. He wanted her in his house. He had but little to say; there was not much to tell. It was something they had all kept together, it was in all equally.

The buried treasure which she and Andy possess together represents the love that they have cumulatively built up between them, the love which they share jointly "in common keeping." The two pearls are part of the treasure, though Andy has a special right of ownership to these. If he removes the two pearls from the kettle permanently, the treasure—no longer held in common—will become depleted forever and lose its value to Philly. In other words, she needs love in order to be lovely.

She had not heard Andy below for a long time now, and a vague fear began to grow, as if it took a beginning at the top of her head and spread downward. It was a fear that Andy might leave her, that she might go forward in life alone, that he might have taken a part of what was in the kettle and gone away. She knew that he would not take all, that his hard and just feeling would require that her part would be allowed. She saw her life spread before her in desolation, the farm empty of life, sunk under the hard, sterile rock of the earth. . . . He might go, she contrived, might have already gone. He might have left the whole of the kettle, not wanting the burden of it.

Thus, with the climactic discovery that the kettle is no longer buried under the hearth, Philly sees "a vacant world stretched out in all ways, as if the walls of the house and all the air and the ground were taken away." With the treasure missing, the world comes apart for Philly. The inner loveliness which she had felt, glorying in the shared love between herself and Andy, is shattered:

"It was such a pretty kettle, filled up to the top," she cried. . . .
"I'm some old crooked woman that lives in a poor old torn-down house. And Susie and all the rest are dead. . . . Oh, God's pity on me! I've lived a hundred years already. . . . And I'll live a hundred more, old . . . and life is hard-to-get . . . hard to keep . . . hard to get shed of. . . . No need to think again about the pretty part . . . weddens and a bright dress for a girl to wear . . . yourself or any other. . . . Oh, God's own pity on me! No little pleasure for myself and ne'er a thing to give to any other. . . . I'm as poor as ever I was, and poorer. . . . We are a poor old man and woman, poor together. . . . Oh, how poor I am!"

It is clear that Philly's "poverty" and "ugliness" are here qualities of the spirit; and the buried treasure, ripped out of the Blair cornfield, is meant to signify that nontangible wealth of human love and companionship so integral to Miss Roberts' thought. The relationship of sexuality to love seems to be indicated by the male and female phallic shapes of the symbols—the two pearls and the ovular iron kettle.

The relationship between sexual love and death is also pointed to in the Ben Shepherd subplot; there we see Ben's dim realization that the dead—the bleached random bones of the graveyard—were once themselves vital human beings, bursting with blood and imposing on the generations to come their heritage and their bone structure. The very fact that the kettle of gold had been placed in the middle of the long line of Shepherd succession is testimony that these bones once accumulated their own buried treasures. The minor theme of the treasure residing in the earth and the generations of men who have tilled appears in the very first paragraph of Ben Shepherd's opening chapter:

> The land rolled forward toward the harvest, or it rolled backward toward the time of planting, toward the long sequence of harvests and plantings, moving backward, over and over, the soil turning, revolving under the plowings of many springs. Back further toward the trees and the uncleared forests, or forward swiftly to the acute moment, the fine and most immediate present, where a man draws a reaping machine out of the barn . . . saying, "In three days, or a week at the longest, we'll begin to cut, if the signs hold good."

From Ben Shepherd's point of view, the kettle of nineteen hundred gold coins is the product of the "long sequence of harvests and plantings" coming to light in "the acute moment." Thus we have represented two kinds of vision—the subjective, caught-in-the-event observations of Philly Blair, and the objective, above-space-and-time view of Ben Shepherd.

We meet Ben on a pilgrimage to find himself, since he enters the Pigeon River country intent on visiting the land that his ancestors had settled, and "he had dismissed from his mind much that he knew of the world by the way of his own lived past, and as he stepped . . . he viewed with pride the fine void he had brought to his memory. . . . He had wanted to become nothing so that he might then try a new way of being." He, like Jeremy, is eager to know answers, to discover "from-whiches and toward-whats":

He followed the droop of the land as it sank and rose with the turnings of the creek, and now and then the vague and continual query that haunted his mind would take the form of some stated question, as "Where?" or "Why?", or "How is it thus?" As if the land had in him become conscious, as if it would ask these things.

His role is that of the student—young, impetuous, a little pompous in his unattained maturity, but eager to examine and to learn. He is amused and intrigued by the discovery of the gold in the Blair cornfield, having secretly watched the scene, but he discovers for himself the second "buried treasure" in the novel—the graveyard of the Shepherds: "The richness of the burying-place in its multitude gave him a new sense of the country as it spread here and there beyond his ledge, as if the people had become a florescence that arose with branchy stems and wide flowerings that reached into every hollow and spread up over every hill, dividing again and again." The life urge which these buried bones once possessed has cleared and tilled the land and peopled it with all its inhabitants. Ben Shepherd himself, like the iron pot which was dragged out of the earth into "the acute moment" after lying dormant for many generations, is a product of the earth —seven generations removed from the original Tobias Shepherd, but formed and shaped by him and all the descendants of him. Ben removes a bone from the burying ground as a

109

reminder of his heritage, and, fittingly enough, startles a pair of lovers in the brush as he leaves the graveyard:

> The lovers were gone quickly, but in the moment of their staying they had been abundant in life and feeling—words, hands, arms, cries, senseless phrases that were heavy with their meanings. They had made the flesh that would stand about the white, hard inner shapes, and in them it was quick and full. . . . He was abashed at what he had seen, and confused.

This swift juxtaposition of death and young passionate sex confuses him with its violent contrast, and later when the girl he has surprised in the graveyard refuses to dance with him, his anger is only partly at the rejection. He resents also the irreverent intrusion of sexuality into the burial ground of his ancestors. His note to her, to be accompanied by the metatarsus, is a double-edged reminder of the scene in the graveyard: "You have got a proud back and a pretty face. Mr. Stoner says you are my cousin ten steps removed or more. You do not want to dance with a wraith now, but some day you may need to. I recommend on that day this bone." But as he enters the busy life of this community, Ben begins vaguely to sense the correlation between the needs of the teeming earth and the sexual love of human beings, reflecting on the people about him:

> They, these people, in the marriage license and out of it, seemed larger and more full than himself, more full of risks, having strange wants and curious needs in their members. Imogene seemed the most rich in this. It seemed to him, dreaming, that it would be a pleasant thing to load risk upon her, to lavish, to spend, to take, to pile up, to make her the earth itself, to give to her, to plow her deep, to plant her with a harvest, to fertilize her with rain, to fling himself down on one of her cool hills in the shade.

110

Elegant Chambers

These themes are joined in Ben's meditation as he listens to Stoner's reminiscences:

They made, all together, a long thread of life, reaching from the birth in the fort downward. The succession of grandfathers spread back and forth through time, they being old flesh, knotted, bone-infested, hard, crooked, and dried out. It was difficult to think of them as having been at any time small and new-born, fresh and young and increasing. They were going, withering, becoming less, and they turned—a complete succession—into random bones, into branching, stony spines of one calcareous matter. . . . Somewhere in the long line thus stretched through time a kettle of gold had been put into the hills, in the middle of them, no doubt, as if one tied a knot in a thread to say, "here," to say "at this point". . . . Ben had a sudden flash of life spring within him, as though in Imogene he were living again.

The long line of his ancestral dead—which in his youth he cannot imagine except as old, inanimate bones—becomes somehow connected to the youthful burst of life which he recognizes in Imogene. For a moment he returns to the mood of his note to Robbie May:

They would be turning about in the same dance to the end of the earth. A bone rubbing upon bone. A bone hurting a bone, wanting a bone, shapes filched out of the clods and set up in life. . . . The senseless sunshine slanted under the trees . . . and the hard light lay over the front of the house. The senseless cloth of their garments stood up before the trees and their nakedness itself was clothing that hid only a little of their inner uselessness.

But this attitude does not last long. Working for the rest of the week in the rhythm of the harvest, he comes to a slow realization that the people of Pigeon River are the products of the bones in the graveyard. He is surprised at his earlier

111

desire to hurt Robbie May and he "unsays" the note. Then, at the end of Chapter IV, he makes a ritual journey to the graveyard to return the stolen metatarsus:

There the moonlight came brightly over the stones, and no lettering being required of them, they seemed clear and sharp, as if they told clear legends. He had been into the homes of the living Shepherds, they now wearing other names, and he had seen them at their working, their living, their play, their lovings. He had walked through their old orchards and among their bees, and he had stripped their seedling grass and cut their wheat. He had fished in their stream and trapped their game in the thickets. He had surprised them at forbidden love; he had eaten their food; and he had prayed with them in their church. Here there was a gay humor over the stones, for the light of the moon and the waning day met with the whiteness of the rocks. . . . In the small inner glade the daylight and the moonlight were dim, but he found his way, and he laid the bone down in the place where it used to lie.

His "treasure" he finds ultimately to lie within himself: the inherited skeletal structure of the Shepherds, the generative power of man, and a feeling of belongingness not only to the dead whose name he bears, but also to the living, who, being human, are his relatives. Thus, searching for a father in order to discover himself, he finds himself and his fathers within him.

As we have already noted, A *Buried Treasure* was planned in the comic spirit, and we can justly expect the complications to be resolved with traditional alacrity in Act Five's Midsummer Night's scene. The kettle is safe; the reservoir of love which is Philly's right to draw upon for "joy" and "pride of life" has suffered no change. The pearls are also safe; Andy had "lent" them to Hester Trigg, but they are now returned.

112

Elegant Chambers

Further, and in the traditional vein of folk humor, the pearls have been instrumental in smoothing out the problems over Imogene's marriage; Hester Trigg has shown the pearls to Sam Cundy, and Sam's life-denying love for Imogene has been rechanneled in a healthier direction.

In the final scene the action expands into a larger frame of reference, as the young men and girls of the countryside come to celebrate Midsummer Night with dancing and singing. The young people organize a "wheel-dance" and play "drop-the-handkerchief" and, in Miss Roberts' description, the mergence into a community created by love[5] and the physical force of sex which serves as a basis for love is strongly implied:

> They joined hands, all in a ring again, and the great wheel began to turn, spread wide to make a moving circle. . . . The great wheel turned, making ready a world, a world of mankind turning all together. . . . As the earth itself the wheel turned under the moon singing. . . . Giles and Imogene were caught now into the fury of the game, for all the young men delighted in giving to Imogene and they were continually tossing the little ball behind her heels. The girls were giving their prize to the boys who in turn gave to the girls, this way and that, and they chased each other around and around on the outer rim of the world, or the great wheel would be turning, making ready.

The force of sex as the power which drives the world forward, which creates generations creating generations, is represented in the metaphor of the wheel turning under the power of the girls and boys chasing one another around the rim. And, perhaps more subtly, the ability to enter into the turning of the great wheel is made dependent on an inner feeling of "loveliness," which can best be attained through the ownership of a buried treasure of shared love. Thus Philly can

113

join the dance and give to the dance, because she has something to give. The novel closes on a note of pastoral harmony:

Philly and Andy started back homeward, down the pasture, driving home the little black calf. The bushes and the briars, the tree trunks and the little saplings, were full of vague, unbodied lovers, and off a little way in the shadows there were these, just out of sight, whispering, under the stones, behind the ditches, under the hummocks. They were all gone from the moonlight and the hilltop.

The world is restored to order and the two buried treasures lie in gentle peace.

Although I have taken pains to analyze the rather complex design of *A Buried Treasure,* I think it is perhaps the least successful of Miss Roberts' novels. The shifts in viewpoint and the complexities of the symbolism are intellectually understandable, but it seems to me that in the reading experience they do not attain that fusion of thing and idea which makes for successful achievement in symbolic presentation. The reader is not inevitably led to connect the Ben Shepherd "treasure" with Philly's iron kettle; he is confused by the prevalence of references to the insect life which likewise abounds beneath the earth. One is never certain whether to take the kettle as an allegorical object designating a fixed human quality, or as an exfoliating symbol which can move through several levels of abstraction. If one is to interpret the kettle in the first way, the range of meanings becomes limited; if one chooses the latter way, the kettle becomes too heavy to move easily from one meaning level to another, and the device takes on a color of contrivance inimical to the successful operation of the symbol.

Perhaps the greatest weakness of the novel is the faulty

integration of the Ben Shepherd plot to the rest of the story. Ben Shepherd himself is a poorly realized character, and although his quest begins positively enough, it fades to a very weak ending. Worse, the significance of his story is never very closely tied in with that of the main plot. It is possible, as I think we have done, to bridge the two plots by analytical interpretation, but I do not think that this bridging is effectively done within the frame of the novel. The characterization of Philly Blair, on the other hand, is one of the fine achievements of the novel, and the presentation of the deep love shared by two very unromantic, inarticulate middle-aged people is both tender and penetrating, and, to my knowledge, unduplicated in contemporary fiction.

A *Buried Treasure* has also something of the fabulous quality of the folktale, creating a world which is illuminated more by the sheen of moonlight than the hard glare of the noon sun, and where a kettle containing gold coins and a Midsummer Night's meadow dance are appropriate symbols. The use of folk material is very fitting in a novel whose theme places so much emphasis on sexuality both as a vehicle of love and as the generative factor in the life of man. The detailed symbolic treatment of sex and its relationship to the organic pattern of Miss Roberts' thought is new in her work, although we can see similar designs operating in her earlier novels, particularly in *My Heart and My Flesh*. The novel is almost, in its largest sense, a lusty paean to love.

However, in the last analysis, A *Buried Treasure* must be regarded as one of Miss Roberts' minor novels, although it is frequently interesting and charming in itself. Here there is nothing of "the colossal, warlike, Homeric, blood-and-anger thrust" which Miss Roberts demands from great poetry. It is, at its best, a playful, pastoral idyll, told with an earthy robust humor and delicate charm; at its worst, it is two ill-connected short stories, forcibly held together by an unconvincing contrivance.

BLACK IS MY TRUELOVE'S HAIR (1938): *The Thimble as Symbol*

MISS ROBERTS' LAST NOVEL, *Black Is My Truelove's Hair*, was first written as a sketch for a short story, tentatively entitled "Tamed Honey," in the spring of 1933. In *Black Is My Truelove's Hair* she turns away from the cosmic scope of *He Sent Forth a Raven* to deal, as in *A Buried Treasure*, with more limiting symbols, and to investigate once again the relationship of sexuality, love, and death. Among Miss Roberts' papers there is a very explicit comment upon this novel:

> From the beginning it was assured that the woman, Dena, would have two lovers, and that the first would come to disaster. That the thimble episode would appear as a shadow of the central theme and carry along the design while it (the thimble) became a symbol of the thing lost and the thing at length found. . . .
> The intention was to penetrate an event in all its implications, deeply and more deeply, until it yielded its entire meaning in Time. Langtry is a symbol—He is Death. . . . In contrast with this man of Mystery is Elliot whose mystery is the mystery of life.

For the plot structure of *Black Is My Truelove's Hair*, Miss Roberts returns to the formula of death and rebirth as defined by an unsuccessful, and then a successful, love relationship—the same formula which figured so importantly in *The Time of Man* and *My Heart and My Flesh*. In this novel, however, the story begins after the first event of disillusionment in love, with Dena Janes "walking a narrow roadway in the hour of dawn," returning in shame and disgrace to Henrytown from a six-day sexual escapade with Bill Langtry.

The novel is constructed around Dena Janes' gradual reacceptance into the community and into her own good graces, culminating with her marriage to Cam Elliot. The dramatic suspense of the plot is supplied by Bill Langtry's threat that if she ever takes up with another man he will hunt her down and kill her. The subplot, centering around the gold thimble, is meant, as Miss Roberts points out, to shadow the major theme—the supremacy of love over hate, of life over death. The symbolic thimble, as Miss Roberts, tongue in cheek, has Dena Janes say, is "not a religious thimble," but it is a symbol of the life principle of sexuality. As we have seen in *A Buried Treasure*, Miss Roberts finds in the processes of normal sexuality an affirmation of the development of the healthy spirit, and a stimulation toward harmonious expansion.

The novel opens with Dena Janes' striving to set her life in order, to live "a life to make sense," and closes when the disrupting violence of the Langtry affair has been absorbed and settled into her total experience. The novel focuses, then, on that same phase of development which Miss Roberts synopsized as "Withdrawal—and sinking back into earth" in *The Time of Man*, the period in Ellen Chesser's life beginning with Jonas Prather's desertion and ending with her marriage to Jasper Kent. But in the earlier novel its treatment is basically expository and episodic, and in *Black Is My Truelove's Hair* it is intensive and dramatic.

Herald to Chaos

As a device to accelerate Dena Janes' recovery and to make explicit the symbolic meanings of the novel, Miss Roberts introduces a kind of character new in her work, the rural oracle, Nat Journeyman. He is the fount of wisdom in Henrytown to whom the people are accustomed to turn for advice and spiritual counsel. He is the high priest of love in the village, making his orchard available for young couples in the dark of the evening, and even bringing refreshments to them. Like Philly Blair, another matchmaker and devotee of love, he is childless and, perhaps for this reason, peculiarly sensitive to the needs of the human heart. It is to him that Dena Janes tells the story of Langtry's threat, and it is he who serves as her guide through the worst early months of her adjustment. At times, as is suggested by his name, he becomes almost the personification of the wisdom implicit in a creative submission to the flow of time. He knows that life, like the river which courses along in front of his house, is processive, a continuum; and that the healthiest way to live is to accept the endless motion of life, neither denying the past, nor making restrictive demands on the future. Observing Dena on her return to the village, while he is setting supporting poles under the boughs of his ripe apple trees, he judges her affair with Langtry, not as a transgression of a moral code, but as a natural consequence of excess love:

"The woman and the tree," he said again. His hand lay on the limb that had been stayed, and he began to lower himself on the ladder. His hand on the trunk of the tree, he adjusted another pole that propped a drooping bough. "The woman and the tree. Destroyed by its own abundance," he said, addressing the imperiled tree. "She hath . . ." —he turned the pole about so that it would better support the limb and made the prop secure on the soft ground beneath—"loved too much, is all is the mat-

118

ter." Letting his body down slowly he passed to another tree, where a pole had slipped from its place. This he adjusted anew so that it bore the weight of the too pregnant limb.

That which furthers life seems to him good; the converse, bad. And in this he apparently speaks for Miss Roberts. Walter's rape in *He Sent Forth a Raven*, Sam Cundy's perverted overprotective love for his daughter in *A Buried Treasure*, and Jonas Prather's infidelity in *The Time of Man* are life-denying acts, and therefore evil. But Dena Janes' fault is at worst an error of judgment.

Journeyman is a new kind of character in Miss Roberts' novels because he is strangely within and outside of the action of the plot. He is Dena's confidant; he functions as an involved character in the denouement; he is emblematic of the life principle espoused in the novel; and, at times, he serves as a chorus. It is he who relates to Dena Janes an anecdote which seems to be intended not only as a clue for Dena's understanding, but as Miss Roberts' parable on the human condition:

"It was a sea bird, lost on the land. I tried to write a poem about it. But one day it shrieked a sudden wild cry and went off into the air with a great sudden flip-flop of wings."

"It was long ago, I reckon," she said.

He flung up his right hand in an angular gesture. "Trapped by life, but not trapped, by God."

"Who is it?" she asked him.

"Myself is meant."

Journeyman would have been entirely out of place in either *The Time of Man* or *The Great Meadow*, but in the folk-ballad atmosphere which its title suggests, *Black Is My True-love's Hair* absorbs him easily.

Herald to Chaos

Miss Roberts portrays Dena's subtle progress toward reharmony with herself, while at the same time showing her continued semi-isolation from the community as a whole. That almost mystical mergence into nature which Miss Roberts seems to have thought of as necessary for making whole a wounded spirit is represented in this novel by Dena's naked sunbathing:

> She turned about, flinging herself over with one agile spring. A faint froth of cloud lay to the right of the sun now. It was less in density than the spider's web and lay in a crescent design that changed from moment to moment but did not float away. Some buzzards went slowly over. She could see the frayed ends of their great wings, and knew that they floated above while they watched her curiously to see if she were living or dead. "They would want me to be dead." . . .
>
> She turned her right side to the ray and stretched out her thighs. She looked slantwise across the tender grass beyond her face and saw a ladybird beetle clinging there. It was vivid red spotted with black. A sweat-bee hovered and darted near her ankles. Far away a donkey jack brayed a long slow two-toned cry that rose and fell. The sun was furious now with heat and light. It was terrible to see. The great reach of the day was but a medium now in which the sun's terror and beauty were set.

Thus, Dena "had been born again into the sun."[1]

But although she has made great strides in reordering her sense of herself, she is still beyond the pale of the community's life. The attitude of the community is represented in the too-forward advances of Ollie McClark, the hired hand on Fronia's farm, who approaches Dena as though they had some secret understanding between them. At the carnival with the Careys, Dena finds that she is excluded from the teasing and dancing of the younger group. She sits with Mrs. Carey, "as if she were a woman a long while married." We see that the path she has to follow is indeed a "narrow" one, and there is no way of changing it except through patience and time.

An omen of foreboding is used recurrently throughout the rest of the novel to recall Bill Langtry's threat:

> While she waited . . . she heard as if it were near at hand the bark of a dog. . . . This bark or burst of tone had a curious timbre that made it not entirely the bark of a dog, but somehow the hoot of an owl was put into it. The sound came in sudden starts, as if a dog had made it. It was a nasal "hoon hoon hoon hoon" in which the sound of the *n* was distinct, but it seemed to be far away. . . . The hoot of an owl came within the rhythm of a dog's bark. Once she decided that it must certainly be an owl, that there was no dog sound in it. It seemed shadowy and near at hand, or clear with remoteness. If it were far it seemed to be a dog, but near it seemed to be an owl. It filled her with a vague apprehension and she went swiftly indoors.

This "owl-bark" is used effectively as an ominous leitmotiv. The grotesque fusion of a dog with an owl, suggesting a perversion of the natural order, gives an effect reminiscent of Elizabethan signs and omens. And like the use of Nat Journeyman, the device fits organically into the tone of *Black Is My Truelove's Hair* because, as Patricia Palmer points out, "The story lives in a poet's world, a country of light and shadow, stillness and music."[2]

The significance of the thimble is described in Miss Roberts' notes as follows: "The thimble is a symbol. Compared more than once to a silo tank, a great round tower that stands beside a barn, it here assumes great size and importance." The thimble originally belonged to Minnie Judd; Fronie had demanded it from Sam Judd as a present, in preference even to a seventy-acre farm. It is not, as we have said, "a religious thimble." Fronia's description of its decoration refers to "little heads that remind me of owls." And Dena, beginning to sense the importance of the thimble for Fronia, pictures the thimble as an item of value outweighing even seventy acres of good bottom land:

Lifting up her head from the hoeing she saw the thimble standing against the sky beside Judd's barn on a distant hill toward the southeast. It stood as a great tower of metal that was gray in the bright sun and green in the shadow, and she heard the plovers from the river shrieking over it. . . . At the base of the thimble-silo stood a thicket, which was the growth of a near fencerow that stood against the thimble in the picture as it stretched broadly from her. She could not see the owls in the bushes among the crossed sticks of the tangled mulberry shrubs, but she thought of them as present and sleeping among the dense shadows of the green boughs.

The phallic symbology of the thimble is suggested in its shape and in its associations with fertile growth (the silo as granary, the owls, and the matted undergrowth), as well as the connotations placed on it through the method by which it came into Fronia's hands. Fronia without her thimble is like Philly Blair believing that the iron kettle of gold coins is gone, except that Fronia is determined to recover her treasure:

She [Dena] herself lay naked in the sun. But this loss and search brought Fronia to a new and a different nakedness. Sometimes it would seem as if all the hidden and inner parts of a body had been brought out to view. Fronia's nether garments seemed to fill the entire yard when they were hung on the line to dry, and it was as if the woman herself were reduced to a few large bodily elements and acts and these were propped up on the clothes poles . . . to offer themselves to the sun and the wind.

Elegant Chambers

Or again, there would be Fronia's newer beauty flowering, a misty light in her eyes and a half-smile about her mouth, and it was as if she weighed today against some other day and made a subtle decision or agreed with Fate to let Chance come as it may and to let beauty take her wherever it would since she had lost the prettiest thing that ever she had owned.

But although the thimble is Fronia's, we must not forget that it is Dena who has actually lost it, and it is Dena who has given profusely of her youthful love with no return. The loss and search for the thimble is paralleled by Dena's movement toward a love which can be shared in a positive life direction, and plot and symbolic subplot converge when Cam Elliot returns the gold thimble to Dena Janes in the heart of a cabbage.

Cam is portrayed, as Miss Roberts suggests in her quoted comment, in antithesis to Bill Langtry. Langtry is a dark, mysterious, handsome man, with no roots or attachments:

A large, gaunt man, of uncertain youth, being of any age between twenty and thirty-five. . . . A handsome smile broke the shaping of his large face into five deep furrows that twinkled and sopped in and out. His great mouth opened and met two furrows at the corners and became dripping wet. Eyes suddenly hard; there was a piercing weariness gathered about the mouth. Then the smile again. Dark locks of hair tossed uncertainly in the brilliant afternoon light. A hand thrust from right to left smoothed the hair to the blackness of the crow's feather.

Although he receives a wedding cake from some relatives to present to Dena, he cannot be defined in terms of a family or a place; he belongs to nothing, as he himself says: "When you hear about old Bill again you'll hear, I expect, he's gone. Lives noplace. Home is where his hat falls off at bedtime." Cam Elliot is quite the opposite. He belongs very deeply

123

to his family, to the land on which he works, and to the community of Henrytown, which knows his habits, his background, and his probable future. Where Bill Langtry is imaged in black, Cam is pink with life:

Shyness gathered about his eyes on the freckled skin. He seemed hot and full of life, and an amiable pleasantness kept continually under his skin, under his eyes, in the lift of his hands, as if he entered pleasure easily and this was every man's right. His face was flushed to a more deep pink. He looked aside from her [Dena] and moved nervously, but he was amused too and this came swiftly to flower even while he bit downward at the corners of his mouth. . . . Firm red life seemed to throb and beat under his flesh in the hand that was raised to brush lightly at his throat and settle at the collar of his garment.

Both men are elusively mysterious, but Langtry's mystery is that of death, while Cam's is the mystery of life.

Miss Roberts evidently placed considerable significance on the episode of the screaming gander, ousted from his flock by Fronia's gander, Old Charlie. In her personal notes she writes: "The Screaming Gander. . . . A part of the great body of Man's woe . . . the principle of unrest and protest. Man protesting his fate. Man bursting the bonds. Man unwilling to stay fixed in his ordered place." Since one of the titles which she contemplated for this novel was *The Lady and the Gander,* I assume that the fate-protesting gander is meant to strike a parallel with Dena's excursion off "the narrow roadway," but I do not believe that the attempt was successful. The senseless shrieking of the gander and the overall grotesque humor of the episode are not sufficiently tied in with Dena Janes' predicament to add an appreciable level of insight to the thematic development of the novel.

Another interesting characterization is brought into the

novel to qualify Miss Roberts' concept of "belongingness" versus isolation. Nannie Bowers, who runs the telephone exchange, is a character in complete harmony with herself and the outside world. And yet she is presented in terms of almost absolute unattractiveness, self-isolated in her narcissism, even though she is at the center of community life. She is one of the self-righteous who reminds Dena Janes of her sinful behavior:

> When she had asked this [an insulting question about Langtry] she knew that she had put Dena outside the bright circle that surrounded her own being. Delicately lustful, she placed the red fingertips along the plugs and made three connections while she answered an inquiry and chattered a moment with a farmwife. She had left Dena outside thus. Plugging thus at the switches, she made a connection and another while she spread her silken legs from beneath her bright dress and turned her white hands about to feast her lover-eyes upon her own person and to enhance her being, assuming now both the seeker and the sought and turning all back upon herself in warmth and conceit. Dena was cast out altogether.

This is, as in the case of Sam Cundy, another kind of perverted love—not outward-going, but inward-doting. We see from the richly connotative imagery that Nannie Bowers has left "the narrow roadway" just as surely as the three vagabond women whom Dena met on her return toward Henrytown.

By using the age-old machinery of the coincidentally lost and found (compare the Cinderella story), Dena Janes is brought to the brink of a rebirth into life. But just as Theodosia Bell was forced to reexperience her vision of Hell before she could give herself completely to Caleb Burns, so the reiterated sound of the "owl-bark" gives warning that the Langtry episode must be fully exorcised before she can become completely whole again:

Night grew into the twilight. She pumped water for the uses of the morning. She fancied a distorted creature having the head of a dog and the body of an owl. It perched high up in the great poplar tree in the great shadows there, all day, but at night it flitted lower to open its terrible dog-mouth and cry owl-cries mingled with dog-rhythms. In the cry was printed the shape, the threat, of the terror. In the five or six notes of the whole cry there was a curve that made a shape as it outlined the iron weapon she had drawn in the gravel of Journeyman's path.

When she has faced Langtry, who fires at her but at the last moment finds himself unable to murder her, Dena walks slowly home, keeping persistently to the center of the narrow roadway which it is her lot to travel:

She went evenly forward, up the small rise and around the faint curve where the way gave slightly toward the right but veered back and rejected the curve thenceforth, as if none had been. The lane closed about the sound of her feet and muffled this to one step and a step, that went as a solitary tread along the narrow roadway.

Black Is My Truelove's Hair is thus, on the level we have been describing, a rather simple pastoral tale of a girl's readjustment to life after the deranging experience of an unsuccessful love affair.[3] However, several elements in the novel, as well as Miss Roberts' comment in her journals, suggest a more complicated intention. On the primary level, Bill Langtry's threat and reappearance have all the marks of melodrama, and the incessant coupling of Langtry and death is incompatible with the tone of a pastoral romance. The

126

following passage, for example, where Dena remembers in painful detail the events of the preceding summer, has overtones of more subtle meaning than is immediately apparent:

It was all very long ago now and forgotten. She had lived again, renewed. Her thought made a summary of the former summer. Dressed up and standing alone the man had been like a great man such as an orator or a statesman about to speak of some weighty thing. He was like a monk. How like a monk? She questioned this decision. Thus when he stood off and apart, his shoulders stooped. It was as if he said prayers. . . .

"It's a strange thing. Sometimes it seems hard to know whe'r I'm here and it's now, or last year and someplace else. And where I was then I can't always tell in a handy way. It was a dream I went into, maybe, or a dream I'm in now. But last year seems real, as real as day itself."

It seems to me that the dream quality to which Dena Janes refers pushes the meaning of this apparently simple folktale to a deeper stratum. If, as Miss Roberts suggests in her notation as well as in the text of the novel, Bill Langtry is a symbol of death and Elliot a symbol of life, then it is possible to read this novel as a symbolic examination into the same area of death and rebirth which we found in *My Heart and My Flesh*. Dena has had the most intimate contact with death, surrendering herself completely to its embraces; suddenly, at the last moment, she rejects death and turns toward life. The action of *Black Is My Truelove's Hair* elongates in time the vivid moments of Theodosia Bell's resurgence toward the life impulse, drawing the action over a one-year period.

It is important to realize that Langtry and Elliot do not pivot on a simple good-and-evil axis. The only absolutes which we have found in Miss Roberts' work are death and life, good and evil being too intricately commingled to be wrested apart. In the following description of Langtry, this mixture is apparent:

A great head of black, shaggy hair that would scarcely stay in form stood firm in the spread image that merged now with all that she did. One great pointed lock fell forward over the forehead. The head was beautiful, and the eyes were troubled or kind. She had never found out the whole of it or entered the mystery. There were three long furrows in the flesh of the face. The mouth was beautiful in its faint smiling. The two deep indentations at the sides of the mouth gave a sharp point to the smile and turned it about over the gaunt face. The smile took her into itself and bathed her in delight.

And it is significant also that the faculty which embraces life is the same as that which embraces death—the faculty of outward-going love.

With this in mind, the following passage, which occurs after Langtry's gun has been smashed and buried, takes on far-reaching overtones of implication:

"Ask her," he said. He too spoke to some other, the invisible or absent, "if she will shake my hand and say good-by to me."

"No," Dena said, speaking slowly, "I will not do so. I will not take his hand. Maybe a long while from now, if he comes, I will shake his hand and speak to him so."

There seems to be an implicit realization that death is eventually inevitable; that, indeed, on some day it will be welcomed with love and longing, even as Whitman croons amorously to "sweet, soothing Death." If this is so, it seems somehow fitting that *Black Is My Truelove's Hair* (and both Langtry and Elliot have black hair) was the last novel which Elizabeth Madox Roberts lived to complete.

CHAPTER FIVE

A Few Hard, Tender Sayings

She tended the housekeeping or wrote fragments of herself on-to fragmentary sheets of paper, rhythmic lines and half-rhymed experience, drawn down into a few hard, tender sayings.[1]

ALMOST WITHOUT EXCEPTION, every literary review or critical analysis of Miss Roberts' work makes mention of her prose style, the inference being that somehow or other, her "style" is an element in her writing which thrusts itself obtrusively on the reader. Even those critics who make more than a superficial attempt to analyze the stylistic devices which Miss Roberts employs fail to integrate their analysis with the functional intention of this style. They forget that "style" is not an isolated segment of a piece of writing, but that it pervades the entire shape of the writing, integral to that shape at all points. This is true, I suppose, for all writing, but additionally significant for an author who is so persistent in her avowal of aesthetic organicism. Thus, a critical comment that "Miss Roberts is fond of Fra Angelico, and her style often mingles the Italian's blues and golds"[2] is of some biographical interest, but hardly helpful in evaluating the quality of her work. To try to go beyond this kind of impressionistic critical reverie which implies that "style" is something like the frosting on a cake, we may begin with Mark Van Doren's astute perception: "her style being most clearly the expression of a mind which is interesting in its own right. Her style is worth discussing because it in itself is a sort of substance. It is more than a way of saying things; it is something said, something which would not otherwise have been said at all, something, we suspect, which could not be said unless it were said in this way."[3]

With this attitude toward "style," let us review for a moment the kind of stylistic problem with which Miss Roberts was faced. We have seen that for Miss Roberts the interest in life is not focused on the external world of things, but on the inner world of sensations becoming ideas. The balance which she tried to attain between poetry and realism requires the literary existence of an active, perceiving, remembering, willing, imagining mind expressing its ideations through sensuous symbols and images. And the "style" which is reflective of such a mind will tend more to the characteristics of lyric poetry than to what is generally regarded as novelistic prose. To take an extreme antithetical example, the modern "hard-boiled" realists, who take their accents and rhythms from Hemingway, have a very different stylistic problem. Since their accent is on the physical causation of sensation, they tend to minimize the creative potential of the mind; the world of things is presented as

A Few Hard, Tender Sayings

fixed and absolute, and the human condition is, in varying degrees, determined and doomed. The style which results from this kind of philosophic perspective calls for clipped, staccato sentences, unadorned by qualifying gradations. Flesh is soft and the things of the world are hard, and so action and violent collision become the polarity of the style. Active verbs, interjections, and "tough" vocabulary are the excitement-making ingredients of the prose, and highly dramatic dialog becomes a premium as a technique of setting the human figures apart from the impersonal forces which move them, much as the traditional disciplines of the theater have differentiated between dramatic physical action and the fixed enveloping stage. It is probably with this kind of novel in mind that Alexander Buchan writes: "One concedes Miss Roberts the title of novelist because the title is ample enough, these days, to include almost anything written about incident. In every one of her tendencies of style, however, she does not write novels, but narrative poems."[4]

Conceivably she might have employed the stream-of-consciousness method to give free play to her belief in the image-creating mind, but she found this method unconvincing: "The exact content or condition of the mind could not, he supposed, be reproduced by speech either written or spoken, however broken the jargon or immediate the rendering."[5] The Jamesian novel, on the other hand, which invites the reader to participate in a strenuous exercise of what we may call "the moral imagination," she valued: "Henry James seems to induce many high opinions and varying degrees of inspiration. He is excellent material as offering points of departure for those delvings into meanings and half meanings which we like to make in an effort to enlarge the capacity for experience and to revalue the human race." But it should be

131

obvious that the Jamesian setting and atmosphere would be incompatible with her interests. So committed to realism was she that she rated Dostoevsky's *The Brothers Karamazov* a failure; in her journal she noted that she admired its psychological penetration, but felt that its characters and interplay of action were too unrealistic to capture the reader. Her creation of a successful style, then, may be the pivotal point on which the evaluation of her novels will rest. And her present inferior reputation may be, as Buchan suggests, a result of inadequate critical response to her style: "In the criticisms . . ., much of the failure to understand the books came from a completely vague appreciation of 'poetic style,' and of the skill with which words—the words of narrative and of soliloquy—were combined to create the effect intended."[6]

Miss Roberts' personal solution to the problem of combining realism and poetry in a narrative form is found in her characteristic combination of the traditional third-person impersonal narrator with the autobiographical point of view. To illustrate this, let us examine the opening paragraph of *The Great Meadow*:

1774, and Diony, in the spring, hearing Sam, her brother, scratching at a tune on the fiddle, hearing him break a song over the taut wires and fling out with his voice to supply all that the tune lacked, placed herself momentarily in life, calling mentally her name, Diony Hall. "I, Diony Hall," her thought said, gathering herself close, subtracting herself from the diffused life of the house that closed about her. Sam was singing, flinging the song free of the worried strings, making a very good tune of it.

The first sentence places Diony Hall in a space-time situation, in the act of perceiving and asserting her identity. Thus far, there is no special innovation in narrative technique; the omniscient narrator has merely established his right to go inside the mind of one of his characters and objectively record her mood. The second sentence poses a problem as it moves the focus closer to Diony Hall, transcribes her thought within impersonal quotation marks, and then adds two participial phrases. If the participles are used to modify the subject "thought," the use of the reflexive pronoun "herself" is unnecessarily ungrammatical; and further, the impersonal narrator has surrendered his "objectivity." Continuing with the third sentence, the problem which germinated in sentence two becomes full-blown. Whose perception is it that Sam, while singing, "was flinging the song free of the worried strings"? It cannot be Sam's, because we have had no preparation that would justify thrusting his sensibilities abruptly into the scene; if it is the narrator's, then the narrator must be a character involved in the action to some degree who acts as a sympathetic storyteller and has a very subjective angle of vision. If it is neither Sam nor the omniscient third person, it must be Diony, but there is no connective link between Diony and the descriptive phrase. As we read the passage over, and especially as we continue reading, we discover that the perception was Diony's, although it has been appropriated by the narrator. Miss Roberts' impersonal narrative voice and her heroine Diony have identical attitudes of perception, imagination, and sensitivity.

In order to perceive this more clearly, let us examine several sentences at the beginning of Chapter III. Berk Jarvis has asked for permission to marry Diony and carry her with him into the wilderness of Kentucky. Thomas Hall, Diony's father, has violently refused to let her go, and has gone to the smithy to take out his anger on the blacksmith's anvil.

The blows on the anvil had become little and thin, put there by a careful hand, and between each stroke there was a long pause while the hand waited on the reflective part of a man. Noon had passed and the odor of cooking foods floated through the room, the dinner being prepared in the kitchen. The day outside was warm in the sun, but within the coolness of the morning still lingered and the dull embers gave out a subdued warmth. Diony scarcely lifted her gaze above the globular billows her skirts made. . . . The anvil had left off its outcry altogether, and presently her father's broken step came on the stones behind the house and he was heard asking for her at the kitchen door.

At first glance the above passage seems traditionally realistic and objective in its presentation. Three sensations—sound, odor, and thermal touch—are recorded, and then the main character is visualized. But if one reads the above passage substituting the pronoun "I" for Diony, and making the appropriate changes in the personal pronouns, the identification of attitudes between Diony and the narrator becomes quite apparent. Nothing is perceived that is beyond Diony's field of perception; all the metaphorical content ("the blows . . . little and thin," "anvil's outcry," "father's broken step") is such that Diony alone could have thought of these things in this way. The verb forms in this passage are also characteristic: "had become," "had passed," "being prepared," "still lingered," "scarcely gazed," "had left off," "was heard." The imperfect tenses and the adverbially qualified past tenses place the action in a limbo of time between present and past; it is action just being completed. The effect is one of immediacy, but an immediacy slowed down to a point where we do not actually hear the blows on the anvil, but we do hear the echoes. The verb forms also create through their accumulation a sense of anticipation, muted, it is true, by the rhythmic fall of the cadences. This anticipation directs itself toward the main figure, Diony, as though the verb forms were animated sensations and were marching toward the human character to be perceived.

The function of this narrative technique is to enable Miss Roberts to tell her story in a loosely realistic frame, while giving her ample latitude, at the same time, to let the mind of her main character order the details of the action. There is literally nothing, no detail, in *The Great Meadow*, which is not under the direct perception of Diony Hall, and yet the novel has been acclaimed as our finest historical novel.[7] When this technique is working well, it is a perfect instrument for attaining "precision in rendering sensuous contacts"; when it is working not so well, it can be a source of confusion and, sometimes, even preciosity. Its limitations are rather rigid; only one character can be fully visualized at one time; if more than one is to be fully developed, some such device as the alternating chapters in *A Buried Treasure* must be used. The subordinate characters take on life only when they become absorbed into the main character's field of perception. But that main character can be artistically realized with a fullness unequaled in the more objective techniques of narration. Thus Miss Roberts' comment on Ellen Chesser is one that many readers can share:

Writing *The Time of Man* I saw Ellen functioning in many situations which I did not use in making the design. She was to me always an organic whole, and I should have known how she looked at all periods of her life and how she would react to any being or event, what she would have said in speaking and what she would have felt in mind or senses.

And since we have seen that Miss Roberts' philosophic perspective is based on the mind of an individual human being—"The most continually present integer"—we must admit that no other technique of narration could have been as suitable for her purposes.

However, it should also be pointed out that Miss Roberts' style does more than merely direct the reader's attention to the main character; it is also carefully graded to differentiate that character and delineate character change. In reference to Chapter I in *The Time of Man*, the placing of Ellen Chesser into the medium of the novel, Miss Roberts writes: "The sentences are short, the movement staccato, and beauty and ugliness are sharply opposed, set continually in swift contrast, as is the way in the life of a child." A random paragraph from Chapter I will substantiate this analysis:

Ellen went further up the creek, jumping from white stone to white stone, feeling safe in the narrow ravine hidden among the willow bushes. She heard quails calling over in the fields, and farm sounds came into the hollow, a calf or a mule crying out. After a little she knew that the farmer had come back from church; sounds heard less than felt told her this, echoes in the hillside, screen doors slamming in the right-hand bushes and rocks. She found a dead snake still bloody from his wounds and this made her think of the man Screw had killed—blood and the breath gone out. She turned the snake over and over to see it writhe, pity and wonder and cruelty in her mind. Screw had killed a man. Haldeen Stikes said he had killed two, but you never dared speak of it even if you called it one. Her father had whipped her once for asking, "Did Screw kill a man?"

In this passage the cadences are short and clipped, giving a sense of the immediate rush of impressions that would ostensibly occur in a child's mind. The sensations themselves are sharp and strident, allowing little room for gradation and qualification: the slamming of screen doors, the finality of the bloody snake. The sudden juxtaposition of the serenity of the ravine, the brook, and the gentle sounds of quail with the violence of the Screw memory is satisfying motivated by the transition through the finding of the snake, an episode logically connected with the pastoral beginning and the brutal memory which ends the passage. We also notice the limitations of Ellen's capacity for amalgamating her sensations into herself; they come and just as swiftly they are gone.

Notice the difference in style in the following passage, as Ellen rides with Jasper to their new married home the day after the wedding:

Some little pointed birds in a flock twitted from branch to branch in the sun, and the road went up a hilltop and lay along a ridge where a woman standing by a great gate stopped to watch them pass, her hand stayed on the latch pin. A woman sat before the door of her house among withering hollyhock stems where the road fell gently down to the valley again, and beside the bridge a kingfisher flew from a limb and darted behind the white of a plane tree, the departure of the bird standing out upon the air as something never seen before by man. Ellen looked at her hands as they lay before the folds of her cloak, her hands acutely recognized and the cloak, hardly her own, folded strangely about her, her body stilled and muffled under the strangeness of the old cloak and the kindness of Jasper whose hand touched her sleeve. The day lay outstretched laterally, no marks upon it, and she greeted herself intently.

This is a very different prose and a very different Ellen Chesser, although the narrative point of view and the basic alertness of mind are the same. The cadences are longer and more gentle in their blending one into the other. The sensations perceived are much more subtly colored with gradations of significance. And, most important, the sensations are selected in terms of significant reference to Ellen

Chesser; they are not, as in the former passage, the indiscriminate rush of whatever is in her field of perception. Her combination feeling of beauty and strangeness as a brandnew bride is delicately implied by her attitude toward the cloak and her awed wonder at the beauty of the bird's flight. The two women she sees at their house gates are perceived under the aspirations of her own dream of a secure domestic hearth. And the last sentence, her realization of herself at the dawn of a new life, ties all her other perceptions into a whole. Commenting on *The Time of Man*, Miss Roberts writes: "The drama of the first part is the drama of the immediacy of the mind, the swift flow of impression. This element being used less as the work moves forward, drama is then projected by the use of dramatic dialogue." The stylistic devices of *The Time of Man* can thus be seen as very conscious attempts on the part of the author to make her prose functionally implement the development of her character, while moving the action of the novel forward as well.

Like her narrative technique, Miss Roberts' sentence structure is organically related to her philosophic and aesthetic perspectives. In what is easily the best critical analysis of her style, Alexander Buchan points out: "Her favorite sentence is simple, a plain subject-predicate assertion followed by a participial construction. . . . When the participle is used not only as a connective, but as a substantive . . . the style appears to move across a regular succession of *-ings*."[8] In the opening lines from *The Great Meadow* quoted above, there are, counting the rhyming words, fourteen *-ing* sounds. These, of course, are unusually frequent in this selection, but it is true that the characteristic sound of her prose is a muted roll, giving an effect of what both Buchan and Van Doren have called "an agreeable monotony." For example, let us

138

look at the following passage from *My Heart and My Flesh*, which describes Theodosia playing the violin:

> Striving to divide her being, to set bounds upon parts, she would turn a half-whimsical gaze inward as she strove to achieve the singing tone and to bow the indefinite legato. "Does the music come out of me really, out of some inner unit, myself, all mine?" she would question, "or do I simply imitate, skillfully or not, what the teacher does?" She wanted to lay her finger on this integer and say, "This is mine." She wanted to go past the bounding of blood in arteries and the throb of her pride in her grandfather's witnessing of her advancing skill. The tone sang more true and she took a great impatient joy in it, searching, as she was, more deeply for the answer to the riddle. Or, in the coming of Albert into her senses, her questioning thought would swim in a pool of inattention and semi-consciousness.

The participial clauses and the repetitive constructions create a liquid rush of sound, subtly cadenced, beginning *in medias res*, tonally, and drifting off at the end with a kind of sibilant indefiniteness. But although the total effect is one of monotony, there are several crisp phrases imbedded in the passage, which seem to be carefully set off and emphasized by their contrast. To illustrate this, I shall take the liberty of attempting to transcribe this prose into cadenced verse, along the lines of Whitman's *Leaves of Grass*. The result is something like this:

Striving to divide her being, to set bounds upon parts,
She would turn a half-whimsical gaze inward as she strove to
   achieve the singing tone and to bow the indefinite legato.
Does the music come out of me really, out of some inner unit,
Myself, all mine?
Or do I simply imitate, skillfully or not, what the teacher does?
She wanted to lay her finger on this integer and say,
This is mine.

She wanted to go past the bounding of blood in arteries
And the throb of her pride in her grandfather's witnessing of
   her advancing skill.
The tone sang more true and she took a great impatient joy
   in it,
Searching, as she was, *more deeply* for the answer to the riddle.
Or, in the coming of Albert into her senses,
Her questioning thought would swim in a pool of inattention and
   semi-consciousness.

It is quite possible that others would transcribe this passage
differently, but I think it is clear that the prose is subject to
transcription on the basis of repetition and cadenced sound
units. Secondly, it is clear that this combination of sound
units has a musically monotonous flow, rising and falling in
succession, but never falling to a complete finality, or rising
to an abruptly high pitch. And thirdly, I think any transcription would have to recognize the emphatic relation of
the sound units I have italicized to the less emphatic sounds
which surround them. The unit, "This is mine," is quite
clearly the most important in the passage, marking a climax
in the tonal pattern. The other italicized phrases are of
slightly less importance, echoing in a minor key, as it were,
the triumphal major chord of the "This is mine."

The musical patterning of these sentences is clearly
designed to evoke emotional responses which will deepen the
reader's sense of the meaning. Dorothea Brande points toward this in her comment: "This prose is a kind of incantation; the meaning does not reach the reader through his
intellect alone. Mind and emotion are equally engaged."[9]
And, like individual barbs aimed to pierce the reading mind,
the significant items, or "the few hard, tender sayings," in
this passage closely related to Theodosia Bell's attempts toward self-realization, are isolated from the musical monotony

140

of the background. The prose style is thus thoroughly functional in its attempt to parallel the actual process of a mind perceiving sensation, and gradually transforming it into realized experience. And further, through the incantation effect of the prose, the reader himself is drawn into the process, participating in the immediate experience, and emerging, ideally, with a truly enlarged vision and a heightened sense of life.

In her diction also Miss Roberts is consistent to the pattern of thought we have described. She is deeply aware of language as the cumulative achievement of countless generations of experiencing human beings. She was fluent in French, had studied a little German, and was an amateur scholar in Middle English. But her view of words was that of the poet, not the linguist. She writes:

I like to think of the origin of the origin of the word, "the world"—*wer*, the root meaning man and *eld* giving old or age—the long life of man on the earth, the were-eld then. . . . Words are poor dumb things when it is the whole yearning of a race, a kind, that tries to speak, but poor as they are they are our most pleasant toy, our most ready delight.

She can be seen playing with words in the delightful passage in which Jeremy reflects on the insistent love letters he has been receiving from the Dark Lady:

". . . I cannot understand the nature of this torture into which she drives me with her scented sinister invitations and offers of sympathy. Whether her skin is swart or her hair raven, whatever is the power of her darkness, whether it lies in her eyes or her soul or her breath, she is despised for a corybantic quean, a toad-in-a-hole, a spayed orgiastic whop, a strumpet-widgeon. A chuff-cat trull, a cootish doltish drab from a trugginghouse. A lustic

141

lymphy gluttish homager, a slipshod thousandleg, an earthen galleyworm. . . ."[10]

She was drawn to the rural speech of her countryside and the dialect which she so beautifully transformed, not because this speech was quaint, but because it was musical; it was more lineally related to the powerful speech of Chaucerian and Shakespearean England than was her nonrural contemporary American language; and it had the marks of earth experience on it. In the following journal note, remembering a group of composition papers which she once had to correct, she comments:

The papers, in a mass . . . I felt to indicate the soil. These young were lumps of clay become animated. They had the marks of the soil upon them, marks of generations of soil, of closeness to the ground, of the struggle with clods and hard earth. . . . Out of the rocky, strong parts of the county came hard, crude, twisted bitten speech. The richer lands yielded in general the standardized speech of schools and teachers.

However, although her strong preference was for the Anglo-Saxon derivations, she was too much the artist to neglect the advantages of contrast. A reexamination of the passage from *My Heart and My Flesh* which was quoted above will show that the significant phrases are Anglo-Saxon in derivation: "Myself, all mine," "This is mine," "Searching more deeply." There is a fairly large preponderance of Latinate words in the rest of the passage, although not as many as might be expected. Still, the less gnarled words, like "divide," "indefinite," "imitate," "integer," "arteries," "inattention," and "semi-consciousness," offer a polysyllabic liquid vagueness, which points up the spondaic definiteness of the "realization" words. And this, of course, is a functional technique of making diction work in an organic cooperation with the other stylistic devices already discussed.

Miss Roberts' particular preference among the parts of speech is for nouns. Indeed, it is not unusual for her to dispense with verbs altogether, transforming a verb form into a participle as in the sentence: "A woman walking a narrow roadway in the hour of dawn." This habit of Miss Roberts' may be related to the primitive attitude which invests a name with an almost sacred significance, faint traces of which can be seen in the names of some of her characters— Diony Hall, Theodosia Bell, Berk Jarvis, and Luce Jarvis. However, this preference can be more directly related to the importance which Miss Roberts gives to the perceiving mind. Sensations are not significant until they have been realized or re-created, or, to put it another way, the life outside is absorbed within only when it is named. Going one step further, Miss Roberts will combine two nouns, locking them together with a hyphen in order to create a composite noun, without losing the strength of either unit in a prepositional possessive or adjective: "man-pleasure," "Memory-realization," "word-touch." This habit is proportionally more frequent in her poetry, and it may be the result of the influence of Anglo-Saxon "kennings," or the byproduct of her absorbed delight in the poems of Gerard Manley Hopkins.

The effects of her handling of dialog should also be mentioned briefly. Because of her subjective narrative technique, she characteristically employs two different renderings of dialog. When her main character is in a situation of relative stasis, the dialog is conventionally handled, often with brilliance. Thus the scene in which Henry Chesser recounts the story of his life to Ellen and Jonas Prather, or the exchange of lovers' vows between Ellen and Jasper, exhibits a dramatic dialog perfectly compatible with the ordinary third-person narrative point of view. However, when her principal character is apart from the dialog, either because of inner dissociation or incapacity to understand—as in so much of the dramatic dialog of *He Sent Forth a Raven*—the effects brilliantly synchronize with the immediate presentation of a character in the jagged process of developing.

It may be instructive here to analyze a fairly representative specimen of Miss Roberts' dialog to observe more closely the kinds of effects she manipulates. The following is a love scene between Ellen and Jasper in the early stages of their relationship:

"Hear the dogs howl," she said, "off toward Stigall's it is. It's a lonesome sound, like the end of the world. Are you afeared of the end of the world?"

"I feel like I could pick up a hill or I could break open a mountain with my fist, and what call have I got to be afeared of a lonesome sound tonight? But it's a lonesome one."

"Lonesome like doves a-callen in trees to each other. Did you ever in your time hear a dove call and then another one answers?"

"I could pick up a hill with my strength."

"One asks the question, the doves, and then the other comes right along with the next call."

"I could pick up a hill or I could break open a rock with my fist."

"It's the sorrowfulest sound there is, as if it knowed what would come. Fair and sorrowful all together. It calls to mind good times that are lost and bad sorrowful ones, both gone together somehow."

"I take notice of doves a heap in spring. A dove call denotes spring is come for sure, and it's safe then to plant corn."

"And a dove has got one drop of human blood in its body somewheres, they say."

"By spring I aim to find some fields worth a man's strength.

144

A Few Hard, Tender Sayings

I'm plumb tired trafficken about, good land and bad as it comes. I aim to go a long piece from here."

"Once when I was a youngone Pappy went to Tennessee and I saw cotton in bloom. We saw cotton grow."

"I'm plumb tired a-trafficken about."

"Saw cotton a-growen. The people gathered it after a while in big baskets, piled up white."

"We'll go to some pretty country where the fields lay out fair and smooth. A little clump of woodland. Just enough to shade the cows at noon."

"Smooth pasture is a pretty sight in a country, rollin up and cows dotted here and yon over it, red shorthorns and white and dun."

"And you won't say 'I know a prettier country in Adair or in Shelby or Tennessee.' Mountains or not."

"Smooth pastures we'll have."

"Whatever I can do to pleasure you, Ellie. The house like the way you want."

"And the house fixed up, the shutters mended and the porch don't leak. To sit on a Saturday when the work is done. A vine up over the chimney. Once I saw a far piece from here . . ."

The dialog continues, but to no conclusions beyond what is already reached. The most obvious characteristic of the preceding is its powerful musical quality, the repetition of words and phrases which interweave between the two speakers as in an operatic duet, leaving them apart even as it knits them together. Both Ellen and Jasper reveal and maintain their own personalities in their speeches: his, masculine and practical; hers, feminine and imaginative. And yet the dialog which seems to be carried out at cross-purposes succeeds in manifesting not only a tonal, but an emotional harmony between the two. Like the doves to which Ellen refers, one calls and the other answers, and although the questions and responses fail to follow one another in logical sequence, there is a dialectic of communion established between them. And this kind of dialog is admirably suited to Miss Roberts' novelistic needs where physical action is always subordinate to the inner drama of self-realization.

Her use of metaphor is the element of her style most difficult to isolate because it is so pervasive. Since the novels are all narrated through an active, imagining consciousness, expository passages devoid of metaphor are almost impossible to find. Indeed, it would probably be fair to suggest that each novel with the exception of *A Buried Treasure* is a very elaborate single metaphor of the experience of its heroine. The mind perceives by combining its new perception with an older remembered perception, and thus, sound is given shape and color, or shape is rendered in terms of nonphysical description. The chaos of sensation in Miss Roberts' novels is continually being yoked into order by the imaginative capacities of her protagonists, and the rhetorical device which expresses the order is the metaphor. Let us examine a sample prose passage from *The Great Meadow*:

When she awoke the moon had set and the dawn was beginning to light the sky. A planet, performing like a small moon, made a crescent in the east. The birds began to arouse, and the cruel, restless dawn began in the trees, the long slow dawn when the birds were insatiable in their pronouncements. The birds arose above the life of the herbs and declared themselves superior, but their declarations needed to be continual. Diony lay in the soft decaying log and heard the clamor among the birds, feeling the vegetable life awake with the sun, each kind standing still in some lewd demand of the light. She came cautiously out of the log and looked about to discover what way she had come there.

The first thing we notice is that the metaphorical content of the passage is related completely to Diony. The coming of

146

the dawn is described, not in order to describe a dawn, but to expose Diony's feelings as she experiences this particular dawn. Factually we know only that the sun is coming up, the birds are singing, and Diony awakes from her night in the woods. More importantly, we know that Diony feels isolated from this activity of nature. The planet, "performing like a small moon," insinuates the idea of spectacle and spectator, with Diony, the insignificant spectator, lost in the vast amphitheater of nature. The "cruel, restless . . . long, slow dawn" chanted in by the "insatiable" birds dispels the concealing blanket of night which had allowed Diony to curl up within herself and fill her whole world with herself—something knowable and controllable. The dawn is "cruel" because it extends the planes of the world, showing Diony to herself as just another speck in the vast forest. The birds make "pronouncements" and "declarations." They blatantly assert their belongingness to the whole scene with irritating little cries of braggadocio. Even the vegetable life makes "lewd demands" of the sun; it too belongs and is part of the order. Diony is apart from the whole, and this the reader knows only from the metaphorical texture of the passage. This kind of metaphorical writing is, as I said, constant throughout all Miss Roberts' prose, unostentatious, but insistently buzzing at the fringe areas of the reader's consciousness. Indeed, her entire stylistic technique is founded on this indirect metaphorical method of exposition.

Miss Roberts will also, from time to time, employ the more conventional kind of metaphor to emphasize a point, or to shock a reader into awareness, or to vary the pace of her narration. For example, in *A Buried Treasure*, Philly Blair catches her hen sucking on the insides of one of its new-laid eggs: "The day seemed unjointed and delayed. The old pullet had eaten a hole into the morning; she had bitten with her hard bill a flaw into the steady world that lay outside. . . . She had made a crack in time itself and in the illusions people hold together." The same devices are at work as in the preceding quoted passage, but the fused images are more incongruous and direct. Or, in the following description of Dickon the carpenter from *He Sent Forth a Raven*, where Miss Roberts somewhat playfully caricatures the character by expanding the metaphor from a simple descriptive statement to a ludicrously cosmic significance: "There were oaths in his speech. His words seemed to burst from his roughly-shaven face and his stiff throat as if they were pinned together with threats that would crack the day into splinters and rip apart the earth itself."

The test of a novelist's style is ultimately the individual reader's, and the writer who chooses to create a distinctive style will inevitably run the danger of alienating some readers who will prejudge uniqueness as affectation. The effects of style are cumulative; the rhythms of a prose work must sustain a prolonged pattern at the fringes of the reader's consciousness before they can begin to function as an integral element of the total work. Stylistic analysis can only point a direction; it can neither "prove" authoritatively, nor make discoveries. But from this discussion I think we can conclude that the extraordinary degree of functional consistency which Miss Roberts' style possesses serves her aesthetic aim by luring her reader into a participative position, where the reading experience may bring a true enlargement of perspective and a heightened sense of reality.

CHAPTER SIX

Symbols of Experience

A DANGER THAT WE TEND to overlook in literary history is what we might call the fallacy of the repeated judgment. Literary history is cumulative, and its scope is so comprehensive that only a small minority of writers can be freshly appraised or even responded to. Undoubtedly this is as it has to be because of the practical limitations of time and energy, but there always remains the possibility that a superior achievement is unnoticed, that some unique quality is obscured by an arbitrary grouping with inferior works which share superficial resemblances. It is, alas, neither logical nor necessary that truth and goodness will always out, and one of the tasks of literary criticism is humble and continuous self-criticism. A writer can all too easily become categorized, and the category, once established, may frequently speak much louder than the writer's works. I think that in the case of Elizabeth Madox Roberts, the often repeated literary judgment that she is a "regionalist" has performed such a disservice.

"Regionalism" is one of the most vexing of literary terms because, with its heavy connotative carryover from "provincial" and "local-color," it registers an unmistakable literary judgment of "mediocrity" without clearly establishing the criteria for that judgment. When regionalism is mentioned, one thinks of the minor successes of Mary E. Wilkins Freeman or Dorothy Canfield Fisher; one does not think of Emily Dickinson or William Faulkner. Yet the literary employment of the term purports to describe writers or writings inextricably associated with a particular geographical region—so closely associated indeed, that the literary work is somewhat overshadowed by the peculiarities of the region it chronicles. However, all four writers mentioned above are deeply associated with a particular regional landscape possessing particular idiosyncracies and influences; and the latter pair is, nowadays at least, never referred to as "mediocre." Obviously the term "regionalism" must be regarded as something less than definitive.

It is impossible here to reconstruct the literary-critical temper of the middle 1930's when Elizabeth Madox Roberts' work became firmly categorized as "regionalism" in the pejorative sense,[1] but several generalizations may be suggestive. The concept of regionalism was taken over by the literary critic after it had passed through the hands of the geographer, the historian, and the sociologist. It had served the social scientist as a technique of measuring sectional differences within a nation that was extraordinarily heterogeneous in its topography, natural resources, populations, customs, and local histories. At the time when the literary critic appropriated the term, the great debate of the depression years was well

Symbols of Experience

under way—a debate that was tangentially concerned with the pros and cons of the increasing nationalization process that was everywhere evident. Because Miss Roberts was a southern writer—and even more, a "rural" writer—and because the Southern Agrarians were the most vehemently articulate of the antinationalization groups, she inevitably became labeled a "regionalist" by both factions—the one using it as a term of praise; the other, of opprobrium. But in neither case did the term express an aesthetic judgment; it merely asserted the truism that Miss Roberts characteristically exploited the folkways of the region she knew best for the composition of her novels.

It should be clear that every writer—and especially one who works within the mode of realism—must use local materials as the working ingredients of his art. Some writers are interested in absorbing more than one regional landscape, but these—Dreiser and Hemingway, for example—are still "regionalistic" in each individual work they produce. Others like Hawthorne, Faulkner, and Miss Roberts choose to remain more or less with the material that seems—for whatever the reason—most attractive and workable to them. They are not therefore any more regionalistic than the former. If we subscribe to Allen Tate's definition of regionalism as "the immediate sense of life in which a fine artist works,"[2] the term may be a useful tool for criticism; in its more popular and less responsible usage, it may have served to conceal the unique achievements which Miss Roberts' novels represent.

And I believe that not only are these achievements unique, but their very uniqueness may have delayed their proper recognition. We are only now beginning to realize that the American literary tradition differs profoundly from the literatures of every other major contemporary culture. The

American has always occupied a unique situation; he has always been radically alone, unsupported by established schools of doctrine within which, or in opposition to which, he could channel his perceptions of reality. The American writer has had always to be obsessed with the problem of identity, because the fluid society in which he has lived has never been able to offer him an adequate definition of himself. Therefore he has been forced back within himself to find there if he possibly could what irreducible minimum lay at the heart of his being. He has been forced to confront the terrible ambiguity of his own experience and attempt to resolve its disorders within the design of a metaphor. And the resultant metaphors, if they are cast with integrity to the highest standards of art, will inevitably be eccentric and untraditional.

American poetry at its greatest—Whitman, Emily Dickinson, Eliot, Frost, Hart Crane—bears about it the marks of new beginnings, of a new and unique pulse in its deepest rhythms which invites even as it defies imitation. And the same is equally true of the American novel, at its most luminous, a chain of prose poems and romances from Cooper's *Leatherstocking Tales to Light in August*.[3] The great role of society, which is the real protagonist of the traditional European novel, has always been absent from the characteristically American novel; instead, the American hero is set in a vast solitude, confronted by the encroaching forces of nature both within and outside him. The American fiction has ever sustained a much closer affinity with the fairytale, the fable, the ballad, and the myth than with the social novel of manners. And when one recalls the superb cluster of nonnarrative poems which are among the finest achievements of American literature—the essays of Emerson, *Walden*,

Symbols of Experience

The Education of Henry Adams—one can see that this passionate concern with self-definition has frequently created completely new and unclassifiable forms.

But self-definition has never been sufficient for the American writer—not unless the metaphor of self were large enough to embrace all men. The "I" that celebrates itself in American literature utters as its second word, "En Masse," and the value of the self-definition is almost in direct proportion to the intensity of its involvement in the wholeness of mankind. This polarity between the "I" and the "We," between self-respect and "fellowmenship," has continually reflected and given new inspiration to the ideal of democratic individualism, itself a similar paradoxical polarity. American writers have responded to this struggle for identity and cohesion by creating a literature of unique achievements. But unique as these individually are—ranging from the passionately reasoned syllogisms of Jonathan Edwards to the translucent word engravings of Wallace Stevens—there is, it seems to me, a common purpose uniting them and a common function underlying their choice of techniques. Urgently, indeed morally, concerned with an attempt to realize the self, they make their special appeal directly to the moral imagination of the reader, not to his reason, nor to his desire for entertainment. They refuse to allow the reader to keep a distance from the works he is reading; they demand that he participate, that he enter into the life of the poem, and they allow him no peace until he has recreated the poem out of his own experience, discovered its meanings in himself, and discovered himself in his creation of meaning. To be sure, literature in this sense is far from an American invention—one thinks immediately of Laurence Sterne, William Blake, or Emily Brontë—but whereas in other literatures such writers

153

are regarded—and justly so—as eccentrics, in American literature our writers of this kind are "classics." For the American
reader as well as the writer is rootless in a metaphysical
wilderness, and, typically, the great works in our tradition
have as their highest purpose stimulating the reader to
create his own identity and discover his oneness with his
fellow man.

In this literary tradition of artistic transcendentalism,
experientialism, and democratic idealism, Elizabeth Madox
Roberts was deeply immersed—soul, fiber, and bone—so
thoroughly as to be caught up not by an influence, but by a
way of life. In our analyses of her individual novels we have
seen her primal concern with the problem of identity; from
Ellen Chesser to Dena Janes, each of her heroines is sent on
an odyssey of self-discovery only to learn that there is no self
to be discovered; there is rather a self in the process of
creation. And the self that is created is the self that creates;
the two are one—the maker and the made, the poet and the
poem through which he knows himself. Consequently, her
poems—*The Time of Man, He Sent Forth a Raven, Black Is
My Truelove's Hair*—must be responsive as symbolic structures to two different demands: They must for Miss Roberts
be adequate distillations of her own experience; and for the
reader they must be adequate forcing beds for the creation
of his own identity. Her symbolic structures are thus neces-
sarily untraditional and liable to be confused superficially
with something that they are not. But by projecting her own
search for self upon her heroines, and by casting her heroines
in images as remote from autobiography as literary characters can be, Miss Roberts sustains a symbolic device of
expanding consciousness with which both the writer and
the reader can identify. And since the final knowledge

154

which Miss Roberts' heroines learn is the necessity of love in order for the self to live—a love which is based on what man shares most fundamentally in common—the reader is given a free channel to identification with the main character, even as he is being given an opportunity to create his own identity. We have in our discussions of Miss Roberts' novels seen again and again that the basic truth of life for her resides in the simple equivalence of creation and knowledge. To know oneself and to create oneself are the same; both processes of realization impose a design upon the chaos of experience, bitterly limited by the fatal truths of experience itself, but, paradoxically, liberated by the freer truths of the integrating imagination. Whether one labels the process "knowledge" or "creation," the ultimate focus of Miss Roberts' vision approximates what Tillich has eloquently termed "the courage to be."

Among the great writers in the American literary tradition, the one whom Miss Roberts most resembled was Emily Dickinson. Carl Van Doren once described Miss Dickinson's world as one which "at first seems full of abstract terms walking angularly through a curious dance. Soon they are seen to be only the symbols of experience. They are people of her world, in which all thoughts are alive. Everything in it achingly alive."[4] He goes on to describe "the innumerable dramas of the heart and mind which need only pinpoints of room" for their enactment; and he concludes that the eccentric appearance of Miss Dickinson's work notwithstanding, "she did . . . all that any poet can do. Whether a poet's garden is wide or narrow, he must, to be a good poet, treat it as a universe." Like Emily Dickinson's, Miss Roberts' universe is a soul-centered universe, all the components of which make sense, become related into an order, only when they are organized into a pattern by the creatively perceiving spirit. Van Doren's insight into the nature of Miss Dickinson's poetry, which he sums up in the phrase "symbols of experience," holds equally true for the novels of Elizabeth Madox Roberts. We note her journal statement, "I will keep to the truth as I experienced it, for these experiences have become true symbols for me." The symbolic patterns which we have found informing her novels are truly the symbols of her experience, projected dramatically in choreographic patterns of thrust and withdrawal, loss and discovery, death and rebirth.

The American accent on experientialism in the creation of artistic symbols makes Miss Roberts' work reminiscent of many of the classic American masterworks, including the capture-escape patterns of *The Leatherstocking Tales* and *The Adventures of Huckleberry Finn*, as well as the expansion-inversion patterns employed by Hawthorne, Hemingway, and T. S. Eliot. But Miss Roberts' experience was that of a woman, and somehow the grandiose continent-embracing empathy of Whitman, or the cool Olympian abstraction of experience which we find in Emerson, are too impersonal, too dissevered from the routine trivia of housekeeping, gardening, and the sewing basket which is never empty, to symbolize the life pattern of a woman who is trying to build a "life to make sense." But in the poetry of Emily Dickinson we find much to remind us of Miss Roberts' work. The symbols of experience are closer to the bone; the personality of the poet is more secretively domestic, more wholly concerned with intimate griefs and happinesses; and the mind of the poet has that sharp intellectual edge which never allows us to forget that this is the experience of just one human soul, "that a popgun is a popgun, though the ancient and honorable of the earth affirm it to be the crack of doom."

Both writers knew well the insatiable yearning of the spirit to accept no absolutes or limitations to the capacity of experience. Both were drawn to the observation of men under extreme conditions, knowing that truth—if it be anywhere—will show itself in moments of joy or, better, agony: "Men do not sham Convulsion,/Nor simulate, a Throe—" Both writers in their works were fascinated by the puzzling intimacy of life and death; both were urgently aware that life could not be lived passively—that to do so was to sink into death-in-life, to be one of Miss Dickinson's shameful "soft, cherubic gentlewomen." And both writers knew that man must die many times in order to live; that experience always entails risk and pain, but the rewards are integrity and self-growth. Miss Dickinson, like Miss Roberts, was a zealous guardian of the privacy of the individual soul; but, also like Miss Roberts, she knew that this privacy would become a self-imposed dungeon unless it were sometimes allowed to suffer the invasion of "a royal visitor" from the outside. And, perhaps most importantly, both writers were at one in their dedication to the introspective focus—in their faith that the life outside is a wind blowing in a mirror, and that one must search within to find the "internal difference,/ Where the Meanings are."

Ultimately, however, the deepest similarity between the two writers is found, not in their thoughts or their artistic techniques, but in their attitudes as artists. Both lived in a soul-centered universe, and both were constantly struggling to define that magical line which marks "the points where poetry touches life." Both were constantly striving to know —to project creatively out of the inmost spirit to the extremest peripheries that the senses can touch. In a revealing journal notation, Miss Roberts acknowledges her affinity to Emily Dickinson: "And moved out a little closer to the edge of things, as did Emily Dickinson. For what is the white clover to the bee?" Here in capsule is the best characterization of Elizabeth Madox Roberts' attitude as a woman and artist. As the bee absorbs and transforms the white clover into honey, so, she felt, must she live intensely, extracting from her experience of life the bittersweet symbols of value and art.

But Miss Roberts' immersion in the American tradition was much more consciously social than was Miss Dickinson's. Unlike the poet of Amherst, Miss Roberts dreamed the dream of the good society on earth rather than in heaven— even as does Diony toward the end of *The Great Meadow*. Like Diony (and like John Logan Treer), Miss Roberts is persuaded that a society must follow the same principles of growth as a human being—that it can be creative only as it is internally harmonious—that "the kelson of creation is love." In her poem "Conversations beside a Stream," she says that there have been "two great songs in America," one of which is *Moby-Dick*:

> The other by Thomas Jefferson beginning:
>   "When in the course of human events, it becomes
>   necessary . . . to dissolve the political bands . . ."
> Gathers into one fiat the wills, the desires of a people,
>   of thousands of thinking and feeling men,
> One man to himself alone
> Cannot make a song.[5]

The value of such an inheritance as the Jeffersonian dream to Miss Roberts is almost incalculable. It allows her to articulate the existence of a strongly linked chain of cultural continuity; she can appeal directly to a system of values and a process of valuation which are an integral part of the spiritual structure of whatever it means to be "American." She does not have to invent a myth or establish a new frame of reference; she already has an automatic entrance into her readers' minds. And believing as she does that poetry is "a high synthesis of aspirations, of social aspirations, group or human longings, brought to clear statement in terms of beauty," she can direct the focus of her artistic attempts on a meaningful, communal level of shared experience. She can write out of the indissoluble loneliness of her own experience, sustained by the belief that her experience is "representative"—that her lonely song captures the basic melodic pattern of a mighty American song.

And yet it is not surprising that her uniqueness should have been largely overlooked, that her precise stylistic devices should have been regarded as eccentricities, and her dramatic symbols of experience have been misread as bucolic sentimentalities. She has been warmly praised by critics of the antinaturalistic persuasion, but in essence this praise all but states that Miss Roberts "thinks right," and the effect of the praise is more to applaud her good intentions than her distinct achievements.[6] Thus Professor Wagenknecht, comparing Miss Roberts' work to George Meredith's, summarizes his evaluation of Miss Roberts as follows: "It is true, as her special admirers have always insisted, that her kind of poetic insight is the very thing that is needed to save the novel from its exhausted naturalism and sentimentalism, but in her case one may still be permitted to doubt whether further development will be assured until this insight has been wedded to a somewhat sounder narrative method than either writer [she or Meredith] was quite able to achieve."[7] Likewise, Professor Knight compares Miss Roberts' novels with symphonies, commenting on the "tonality of her prose, the development of her themes, and the transition from adagio to finale"; however, he concludes, "She did not realize that the antiphonies of her dialogue become to some readers a tiring mannerism."[8] It would seem that even those critics who admire her work most are fearful of committing themselves to a too superlative judgment.[9] The critics, on the other hand, who do not admire her at all either ignore her completely or consign her to their crowded paragraphs on regionalists and other novelists.

But it may be that the time has arrived for a fresh response to, and a fresh appraisal of, her passionately wrought symbols of experience. In my analyses of her novels, I have attempted to show the process of "symbolism working through poetic realism," which was her own description of her working techniques. I have pointed out that in her four major novels, *The Time of Man, My Heart and My Flesh, The Great Meadow,* and *He Sent Forth a Raven,* she sought to infuse the modern realistic novel with the themes and the grandeur of the classical epic. I think that her success in this attempt may be measured by the impact of these novels; I can think of few other novelists who have more movingly portrayed the epic consciousness of the American experience.

I have tried to demonstrate the functionalism of her artistic perspective and techniques. We have seen that an astonishing consistency of purpose has guided the development of her prose style, characterization, narrative focus, and plot structuring. Consciously or unconsciously, the innumerable details throughout her seven novels are made to reflect directly and indirectly the concept of reality which was most fundamental to her thought. This close functional alliance between the content of mind and the artistic illusion creates a literary

Symbols of Experience

situation in which Emerson's words, "Art is the path of the creator to his work," are incisively relevant; not only do Miss Roberts' novels appear almost as artistic extensions of herself, but they are so constructed as to become for the participating reader artistic extensions of himself as well.

I have also attempted to show the high degree of organic harmony which pervades Miss Roberts' thinking, creating, and, probably, being. We have noticed how closely her thinking in one area is dependent on her thinking in other areas. In her best novels, we saw how this harmony interconnects her use of subplots, subthemes, and great framing symbols. We noted also an organic line of development linking her individual novels, so that we could almost feel the harmonious expansion of Miss Roberts' artistic spirit, as it moved from one problem to the next emergent problem.

In short, I have tried to demonstrate my conviction that the novels of Elizabeth Madox Roberts represent a major contribution to modern American letters—a contribution which is generally ignored or rejected today. Her ability to capture a mass audience, as well as to win critical acclaim, was demonstrated by the substantial success of *The Time of Man* and *The Great Meadow*, but she is no longer well regarded. I cannot explain this fact. It may be, as Alexander Buchan and Mark Van Doren point out, that her poetic techniques alienate an audience trained to read a more naturalistic prose.[10] This may be so, but it is easy to think of other novelists whose style is similarly "poetic" who are not ignored. It may be that her undeserved reputation as a precious, genteel lady writer, stemming from the inevitable "regionalist" tag, has kept away from her work precisely those readers who would be most qualified to be interested in her.

Herald to Chaos

But whatever the reasons for her current neglect, I feel that for the reader who will allow himself to be sensitized by Miss Roberts' poetic prose techniques, for the reader who will participate in her narrative methods, for the reader, above all, who will submit his time and patience to the creative experience of evaluating his own "out-lying spaces" —for such a reader, there is a mine of quality in all of Miss Roberts' novels, and in three or four of these novels, a record of achievement which places Elizabeth Madox Roberts among the finest half-dozen American novelists in this century.

Her deep faith in man and her consistent conviction that all is chaos until it becomes known by the mind—patterned, that is, by the spiritual imagination—makes hers a steady, strong affirmative voice in a world that is clamorous with degraders of the individual human spirit. It is this nonnaive, unsentimental note of affirmation which, ultimately, makes me believe that Miss Roberts' works will survive and grow strong in our cultural tradition. A distilled expression of this can be seen in the poem "Sonnet of Jack," which Miss Roberts chose for the dedication of *Song in the Meadow*, the last volume she ever published. It expresses far more luminously than I can explain her faith in the creativity of life and of man:

Symbols of Experience

I give you day, our day, any day, for entering
Man's time on the earth, his world, for cutting aslant
    through his track
At the crossroads here, bearing his heave-hoe aback,
At the point where his damned-to-perdition sin and his
    sheltering
Spirit join his throat-throbbing, bird-singing
Joy,—here, stubble-wise and tool-handed, into the day
    comes Jack,
Jack Plumber, Jack Plowman, Jack Scrivener, dowered with
    much or the lack
Of it, man-willed, washed up as beach drift out of
    protean weltering.

His friends, then with him, one to pull, take, haul,
    fetch and carry,
Come with himself, no less in the reckoning,—Bob,
    Dick, and Harry.
Or woman-formed, dainty in dalliance or strong in her
    childings,
Kate, Mug, or Prue. They, all, giving God praise, sown
    thus as wildings,
Spread free of the bony house toward heaven, their joy,
    his or theirs, say
What you will,—dead Friday and born again already
    on Thursday.

Selected Bibliography

THIS BIBLIOGRAPHY IS unashamedly restrictive. I have omitted almost all book reviews and glancing surveys in which Miss Roberts' work figures but slightly. I have tried to include everything of any real significance or importance. For a more comprehensive checklist, see the bibliography in my "Elizabeth Madox Roberts: Her Symbolism and Philosophic Perspective" (unpublished dissertation, Boston University, 1957).

ADAMS, J. Donald. "Elizabeth Madox Roberts," *Virginia Quarterly Review*, XII (1936), 80-90. Adams' position, developed in this article, is substantially the same that he has repeated in his *The Shape of Books to Come* (New York, 1944, pp. 125-30) and his preface to Campbell and Robinson's *Elizabeth Madox Roberts*. In brief he holds that Miss Roberts' work is affirmative and universal, and at its best represents a joining of "the fact and the vision." He finds *The Time of Man, The Great Meadow* and *My Heart and My Flesh* to be her best novels, in that order. He sees Miss Roberts as the leader of the group of writers (Pearl Buck, Willa Cather, and Ellen Glasgow) which will raise contemporary fiction out of the "naturalistic morass" in which it founders. In his position as editor of the *New York Times Book Review*, he has been able to argue his position with great persistence and frequency.

ADAMS, J. Donald, and others. *Elizabeth Madox Roberts: An Appraisal.* New York, The Viking Press, 1938. This is an updating of the Glenway Wescott volume of 1930 consisting of contributions mostly published earlier as articles and book reviews. The contributors are Rosamond Milner, Robert Morss Lovett, Edward Garnett, Harry Hansen, Allan Nevins, Carl Van Doren, Harry Emerson Wildes, Mary Ross, Joseph Henry Jackson, and Louis Untermeyer. The articles contain some information of biographical interest, but are in general of slight significance. The Rosamond Milner contribution (published February 21, 1929, in the Louisville *Courier-Journal* as an interview with Miss Roberts) contains some important statements by Miss Roberts on her work.

BUCHAN, Alexander M. "Elizabeth Madox Roberts," *Southwest Review*, XXV (1940), 463-81. This is the best study of Miss Roberts' style as a functional element in the composition of her novels. Buchan demonstrates that her "poetic style" must be dealt with in its own terms or Miss Roberts' intentions and effects will be badly misinterpreted.

CAMPBELL, Harry Modean, and FOSTER, Ruel E. *Elizabeth Madox Roberts: American Novelist.* Norman, University of Oklahoma Press, 1956. This includes and expands on two previous articles by Professor Campbell, "A Revaluation of Elizabeth Madox Roberts' *The Time of Man* and *The Great*

Selected Bibliography

Meadow," Shenandoah, V (1954), 42-59; and "The Poetic Prose of Elizabeth Madox Roberts," *Southwest Review,* XXXIX (1954), 337-46. It is the only full-scale critical treatment of Miss Roberts to date, dealing not only with her novels, but her poetry, her short stories, and her life as well. Professor Foster's biographical chapter offers information not elsewhere available, but since his presentation is in the form of an impressionistic reminiscence, and since he dispenses for the most part with the apparatus of literary documentation, it may be suspected that Miss Roberts' biography is yet to be written. It is possible that Professor Foster's intimacy with Miss Roberts' region may have made him diffident about casting any but a romantic image of her. The analyses of the novels stress the organic unity of her entire *oeuvre* around a major theme, "the primacy of spirit," finding in her best novel, *The Time of Man,* "a poetic regionalism that should . . . have a universal appeal." The absence of bibliography is a major defect.

DAVIDSON, Donald. "Analysis of Elizabeth Madox Roberts' *A Buried Treasure,*" *Creative Reading,* December, 1931, pp. 1235-49.

JANNEY, F. Lamar. "Elizabeth Madox Roberts," *Sewanee Review,* XLV (1937), 388-410. This is a sensitive and frequently penetrating analysis of Miss Roberts' work. It is particularly successful in its treatment of Miss Roberts' handling of nature and her inner narrative focus.

KNIGHT, Grant C. "Bluegrass and Laurel: The Varieties of Kentucky Fiction," *Saturday Review,* January 6, 1945, pp.

Selected Bibliography

12-13. Professor Knight had discussed the fictions with Miss Roberts before writing this brief but significant article. There are very provocative comments on the relationship of music to her work, as well as the first serious attempt to deal with *He Sent Forth a Raven*.

ROVIT, Earl H. "Recurrent Symbols in the Novels of Elizabeth Madox Roberts," *Boston University Studies in English*, II (1956), 36-54. The author's first version of this book.

"She Writes the Way She Weaves," Louisville *Courier-Journal*, January 8, 1939. An extended interview with Miss Roberts of considerable interest as regards her artistic attitudes.

SPEARS, Woodbridge. "Elizabeth Madox Roberts: A Biographical and Critical Study" (unpublished dissertation, University of Kentucky, 1953). This is the most substantial and definitive biographical source to date. It is particularly helpful for tracking down Miss Roberts' many publications, especially her poems.

VAN DOREN, Mark. "Elizabeth Madox Roberts," *English Journal*, XXI (1932), 521-28. This is the first piece of literary criticism to be written on Miss Roberts' work. It calls attention to the aesthetic significance of her style and to the stylistic necessities which her brand of idealism imposed on her work.

WAGENKNECHT, Edward. *Cavalcade of the American Novel*. New York, Henry Holt and Company, 1952, pp. 389-96. A solid appreciative "survey" presentation with bibliography.

Selected Bibliography

Wescott, Glenway, and others. *Elizabeth Madox Roberts: A Personal Note.* New York, The Viking Press, 1930. See note on Adams, *Appraisal,* above. The only item appearing in this that was not republished in the Adams collection was Wescott's "Elizabeth Madox Roberts: A Personal Note," which first appeared in *Bookman,* LXXI (1930), 12-15.

Notes

CHAPTER ONE: Introduction

¹ It is possible that Miss Roberts' critical reputation is moving into a gradually ascending phase. Note the following recent publications: Edward Wagenknecht, *Cavalcade of the American Novel* (New York, 1952), 389-96; Harry Modean Campbell and Ruel E. Foster, *Elizabeth Madox Roberts* (Norman, 1956).

² Miss Roberts' biography is something of a special problem. The source to which I am most heavily indebted is the unpublished dissertation (University of Kentucky, 1953) by Woodbridge Spears, "Elizabeth Madox Roberts: A Biographical and Critical Study." The Campbell and Foster book offers some additional material, but in general this is too subjective and romanticized to be very useful. I have also benefited greatly by extended conversations with Dwight and Barbara Anderson of Louisville; the Andersons were intimate friends of Miss Roberts from 1926 until her death in 1941. Besides the primary sources elsewhere cited, I have had access to the Elizabeth Madox Roberts letters in the archives of the Filson Club in Louisville.

³ The precise nature of her illness is difficult to ascertain. The Andersons conjecture that the disease of her youth was tuberculosis, and there is much supporting evidence for this view. She seems never to have attained vigorous health at any time in her life, suffering constantly from an acute hypersensitivity to cold and to noise. As a consequence of this, she seems to have developed an almost morbid

Notes

fear of any change in routine—a routine, incidentally, in which social contacts played little part.

4 Colorado Springs, Goudy-Simmons Printing Co.; the text was illustrated by Kenneth Hartley.

5 New York, B. W. Huebsch, Inc.; shortly afterward, Huebsch, Inc., became The Viking Press in a merger, and all Miss Roberts' subsequent publications were issued under the Viking imprint.

6 At her death she was well into two major writing projects: a long cycle of poems dealing with the Daniel Boone legend, and a novel based on the Louisville flood of 1937.

7 The Elizabeth Madox Roberts Papers (Bureau of Manuscripts, Library of Congress). These papers include stray letters, newspaper clippings, manuscripts in all stages, and working notes. They extend over a twenty-five-year period in an undated, unarranged jumble. The bequest was made in two gifts, 1943 and 1955, by the executor of Miss Roberts' estate, Ivor Roberts, her youngest brother. Since it is impossible to cite the specific location of material taken from this source, the reader may assume that all quotations of Miss Roberts not otherwise identified appear in this collection of papers.

8 *Jingling in the Wind.*

CHAPTER TWO: Moments of Union

THE TIME OF MAN

1 "Elizabeth Madox Roberts," *Sewanee Review*, XLV (October, 1937), 391-92.

2 "Like Harmony in Music," *Sewanee Review*, XXXV (January, 1927), 104-105.

3 The snug room, the chest, and the key operate also as conventional sex symbols. See the analysis of *A Buried Treasure* for a discussion of Miss Roberts' use of similar material.

4 Reprinted in Glenway Wescott, *Elizabeth Madox Roberts* (New York, 1930), 15.

5 Thus, Harry Bernard (*Le Roman Régionaliste aux Etats-Unis*, Montreal, 1949, p. 89) writes: "*L'intérêt se concentre sur Ellen Chesser, qui aspire depuis l'enfance à sortir de son milieu misérable. . . . Le livre laisse une double impression de beauté et de pessimisme.*"

Notes

For variations on this reading see Kenneth Burke, "A Decade of American Fiction," *Bookman,* LXIX (August, 1929), 561-67; Grant C. Knight, "Bluegrass and Laurel: The Varieties of Kentucky Fiction," *Saturday Review,* January 6, 1945, pp. 12-13; Amy Loveman, "Elizabeth Madox Roberts," *Saturday Review,* March 22, 1941, p. 10; Glenway Wescott, "Elizabeth Madox Roberts: A Personal Note," *Bookman,* LXXI (March, 1930), 12-15.

⁶ Compare the parallel treatment of Dorinda Oakley in Ellen Glasgow, *Barren Ground,* Miss Glasgow's heroine is much more "conscious" and analytical than Ellen, and her "victory" is much more tenuous.

MY HEART AND MY FLESH

¹ Miss Roberts' heroines characteristically project their dreams, or at least those dreams which embody their notions of the good life, in terms of place. Compare Luce's Mome with Diony's vision of the future in *The Great Meadow* and Jocelle's creation of "The Place" in *He Sent Forth a Raven.*

² Vestiges of this plan can be found connecting *The Great Meadow, My Heart and Flesh, The Time of Man, A Buried Treasure,* and *He Sent Forth a Raven.* For example, Luce is the great-great-great-granddaughter of Diony Hall Jarvis (*The Great Meadow*), and Stoner Drake (*He Sent Forth a Raven*) was named Jarvis in the first draft of that novel. See Campbell and Foster, *Elizabeth Madox Roberts,* 281-82.

³ Stiles is engaged in forming a tobacco pool, which would date the novel at approximately 1905, the time of the celebrated Kentucky Tobacco War. Stiles serves a similar function to, and forcibly reminds one of Caspar Goodwood (*The Portrait of a Lady*).

⁴ Miss Roberts has reported that she composed *My Heart and My Flesh* while listening to Beethoven's Ninth Symphony on records.

⁵ *Cavalcade,* 391.

⁶ *Elizabeth Madox Roberts,* 8.

⁷ "Elizabeth Madox Roberts," *Virginia Quarterly Review,* XII (January, 1936), 86. Adams' warm regard for Miss Roberts' work must, of course, be evaluated with a consideration of his equally warm disregard for Faulkner's work.

⁸ *Bookman,* LXIX, 564.

⁹ *Sewanee Review,* XLV, 395.

Notes

CHAPTER THREE: The Outlying Spaces

THE GREAT MEADOW

1 Wagenknecht, *Cavalcade*, 390.

2 See Mary Austin, "Regionalism in American Fiction," *English Journal*, XXI (February, 1932), 97-106; Pierre Brodin, *Le Roman Régionaliste Américain* (Paris, 1937), 116; and E. E. Leisy, *The Historical Novel* (Norman, 1950), 118. *The Great Meadow* was made into a particularly inept motion picture in 1931.

3 With the birth motif in mind, the subsequent death of Elvira Jarvis becomes functionally related to Diony's new emergence as a mature woman, independent in her own right. Thus, after Elvira is dead, Diony continues to catch images of her among the women of the fort, and we can see the ambivalence of her situation in the following: "Then Diony would sink into a web of pain and gratitude, and in the tangle at last some inner spark or motion would arise which wanted to be free of the web and wanted to be of some unity or account in its own right."

4 Compare the following statement by Walter P. Webb: "The American concept holds that the frontier lies *within*, and not at the edge of the country—not a line to stop at, but an area inviting entrance." ("The Age of the Frontier," *Perspectives* USA, XI (Spring, 1955), 55.)

5 Compare with John Logan Treer's similar reflection in *He Sent Forth a Raven*: "I was inside. I was at the very heart of the age, at the beginning of what's to come after."

6 The matter of names is interesting here. On Berk, Miss Roberts bestows the name of Bishop Berkeley, the symbol of creativity in the novel; Evan, on the other hand, may connote "even" in the sense of level, poised, balanced.

HE SENT FORTH A RAVEN

1 Thus, Allan Nevins writes: "As the title indicates, there are perhaps [!] symbolic values in the tale; if so, each reader can apply

Notes

his own philosophy to find them." ("Home in Kentucky," *Saturday Review*, March 2, 1935, p. 22); see also Janney, *Sewanee Review*, XLV, 401; and Wagenknecht, *Cavalcade*, 393.

[2] *Saturday Review*, January 6, 1945, p. 13.

[3] For a somewhat tentative discussion of this theme, see both Adams, *Virginia Quarterly Review*, XII, 84-85; and Janney, *Sewanee Review*, XLV, 401.

[4] *Saturday Review*, January 6, 1945, p. 13.

[5] In the novel her cynical withdrawal from life is occasioned by the dictatorial interference of her father into her illicit affair with the astronomer Wayne. The episode was obviously meant to be of considerable importance to the total meaning of the novel, but as it stands, it is too enigmatically incoherent for complete interpretation. As I read it, Martha is betrayed by Wayne's sterile scientism. He is content to collect measurements of the celestial order without concerning himself with the metaphysical questions of origins and purposes. Stoner Drake senses what to him is a spiritual indifference tantamount to death in the young man and hence expels him from Wolflick as an element of disease (Walter's lust and J.T.'s facile opportunism are likewise expelled). Martha reluctantly accepts Drake's judgment without being able to love the judge who has exposed her own deficiency of evaluation.

Wayne also makes a striking contrast with Boone in *The Great Meadow*. Like Boone, he is "never lost," but his self-possession is the result of his never venturing beyond the frontiers of the known. Paradoxically, his self-sufficiency is achieved through a denial of self —a direct contradiction to the "life is from within" principle.

[6] In the order in which the dramatis personae appear on the scene, Miss Roberts may be suggesting the stages in the evolution of the personality. Will is first and foremost, lasting to the end as a dominating force even as it becomes erratic and aimlessly bewildered. It is followed by duty, the creative imagination, faith, and reason; and it is only after the personality has attained a coalescence of maturity that the ideal of "fellowmenship" makes its appearance.

[7] Miss Roberts' extended comments on the novel, as reported in a newspaper interview, are of interest here: "It has been the fashion to damn *He Sent Forth a Raven*. I have looked it over in tranquility, two years after it left my hands. It is not a fantasy. It follows the pattern of *My Heart and My Flesh* and is more like this work in feeling and structure than it is like any of my other books. The reviewers generally confused themselves looking into the characters

to try to find the Raven. Once they got on the wrong track, there was no finding their ways back. The Raven of the piece is the dauntless spirit of that poor weakling, Man, trying to go his way alone. Old Stoner Drake had a world of Raven-ness in him, and thus he tried to flit to and fro, as is written in the story of the flood, until the waters subsided. But he was defeated in the end by God's weapon of senility; and, in spite of him, God's other weapon, Life, went on functioning in Jocelle and her child. The book did not settle any of the problems of war, they say. Did anything settle any of the problems of war? And isn't the old story still there to be told—of war's futility?" (Louisville *Courier-Journal*, January 8, 1939)

CHAPTER FOUR: Elegant Chambers

JINGLING IN THE WIND

[1] Wagenknecht, *Cavalcade*, 390.
[2] *Saturday Review*, March 2, 1935, p. 22.
[3] *Bookman*, LXIX, 563.
[4] "Society Notes from a State Reformatory," collected in her private papers, exhibits the same kind of heavy overdrawn humor.

A BURIED TREASURE

[1] The novel was first written and published in short story form; see "A Buried Treasure," *Harpers Magazine*, CLX (December, 1929; January, 1930), 1-10, 228-38. It is a highly adumbrated version of the novel, serving as a kind of synopsis to the later work.
[2] Wagenknecht, *Cavalcade*, 390n.
[3] Wagenknecht, *Cavalcade*, 390n.
[4] The number of the discovered coins is probably significant. Nineteen hundred brings irresistibly to mind the age of the Christian era, and we may suppose that the "treasure" symbolism will be interlinked with the progress of modern civilization.
[5] The derivative meaning of "Philadelphia" (brotherly love) is clarified in this final scene.

Notes

BLACK IS MY TRUELOVE'S HAIR

[1] Theodosia Bell undergoes an almost identical cure at Spring Valley Run in *My Heart and My Flesh*.

[2] "A Faraway Land," *Canadian Forum*, XVIII (March, 1939), 382.

[3] It should be noted that there is the inevitable "social" interpretation. Benjamin Spencer ("Wherefore This Southern Fiction," *Sewanee Review*, XLVII (October, 1939), 500-13) sees Dena as an allegorical representation of the South violated by modern industrialism (Langtry), but ultimately victorious through a return to bucolicism.

CHAPTER FIVE: A Few Hard, Tender Sayings

[1] *He Sent Forth a Raven.*

[2] Grant C. Knight, *American Literature and Culture* (New York, 1932), 458.

[3] "Elizabeth Madox Roberts," *English Journal*, XXI (September, 1932), 522.

[4] "Elizabeth Madox Roberts," *Southwest Review*, XXV (July, 1940), 475.

[5] *Jingling in the Wind.*

[6] *Southwest Review*, XXV, 463-64.

[7] Leisy, *Historical Novel*, 118.

[8] *Southwest Review*, XXV, 467.

[9] "Four Novels," *Bookman*, LXXV (December, 1932), 828.

[10] *Jingling in the Wind.*

CHAPTER SIX: Symbols of Experience

[1] See my "The Regions Versus the Nation: The Critical Battle of the Thirties," *Mississippi Quarterly*, XIII (Spring, 1960), for an attempt to make such a reconstruction. For an understanding of the counter positions and the ardor of the struggle, the following are

Notes

helpful: Joseph E. Baker and Paul Robert Beath, "Regionalism: Pro and Con," *Saturday Review*, November 28, 1936, p. 3; Donald Davidson, *The Attack on Leviathan* (Chapel Hill, 1938); and Howard W. Odum and Harry E. Moore, *American Regionalism* (New York, 1938).

[2] Quoted in Davidson, *Attack on Leviathan*, 83.

[3] Three brilliant recent studies which seem to me to substantiate this position are Quentin Anderson, *The American Henry James* (New Brunswick, N. J., 1957); Richard Chase, *The American Novel and Its Tradition* (New York, 1957); and R. W. B. Lewis, *The American Adam* (Chicago, 1955).

[4] *Modern American Prose* (New York, 1934), 913.

[5] Collected in *Song in the Meadow*. It is interesting to note that Miss Roberts' fellow Kentuckian, Robert Penn Warren, seems to find it necessary to abjure the Jeffersonian vision in favor of that of Melville; see especially his *Brothers to Dragons*. Miss Roberts' fundamental optimism can be measured by the fact that without denying validity to the tragic Melvillean perception, she is able to merge it within the comic frame of an optimistic humanism.

[6] Thus, C. John McCole, citing the violence, cruelty, and experimentalism which appalls him in Dos Passos, Hemingway, and Faulkner, contrasts to them the health of the modern "regionalists," among whom is Miss Roberts: "There is no sign of pessimism, defeatism, and despair in all of this! Does it not seem, then, that we must look to our 'regionalists' for that real temper which alone can counteract the literary distemper of our times?" (*Lucifer at Large*, (London, 1937), 200)

For variations of this position, see Adams, *Virginia Quarterly Review*, XII, 80-90; Harry Modean Campbell, "The Poetic Prose of Elizabeth Madox Roberts," *Southwest Review*, XXXIX (Autumn, 1954), 337-46; and J. D. Robins, "Elizabeth Madox Roberts," *Canadian Forum*, XI (November, 1930), 66-67. It is at least worth a conjecture that this kind of fulsome praise may be in part responsible for the neglect of Miss Roberts' work.

[7] *Cavalcade*, 396.

[8] *Saturday Review*, January 6, 1945, p. 13.

[9] J. Donald Adams has been the significant articulate exception to this rule. From time of his 1935 introduction to the Modern Library edition of *The Time of Man*, he has been constant in his high appraisal of her achievements.

[10] Buchan, *Southwest Review*, XXV, 463-64; Van Doren, *English Journal*, XXI, 522-23.

Index

Index